FOREVER HOME

A Memoir

FOREVER HOME

A Memoir

Lorraine Jenkins-Wilkes

Printed in the United States of America

Cover Designer: BVS Images & Designs
Editor: LPW Editing & Consulting Services, LLC

First Printing, 2018

ISBN – 13: 978-0-692-14892-1

Scriptures marked KJV are taken from the KING JAMES VERSION (NKJV): Scripture taken from the KING JAMES VERSION®. Copyright© 1982 by Thomas Nelson, Inc. Used by permission. All rights reserved.

In Honor of my Mother, Mary Rose Jenkins

Thank you, Mama for giving birth to me. I will always
remember your big, bright smile.
I will love you always and may you finally rest in peace.
I am happy that you have found your forever home.

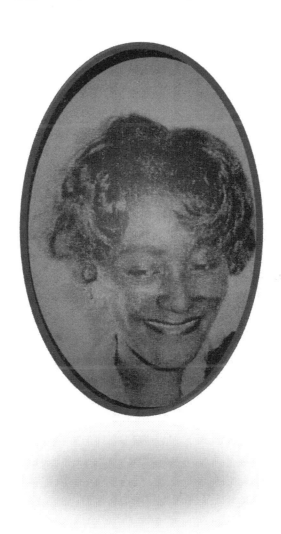

To my LORD and SAVIOR JESUS CHRIST:

Thank You for salvation and delivering me from my past.
Thank You for giving me the power to help
someone else to be free.
Thank you for the courage to write this story.
Thank you for my sisters, who have endured and now have
the power to move forward.

Psalm 24: 1:10 (KJV)

The earth is the Lord's, and the fulness thereof; the world, and they that dwell therein.

2 For he hath founded it upon the seas, and established it upon the floods.

3 Who shall ascend into the hill of the Lord? or who shall stand in his holy place?

4 He that hath clean hands, and a pure heart; who hath not lifted up his soul unto vanity, nor sworn deceitfully.

5 He shall receive the blessing from the Lord, and righteousness from the God of his salvation.

6 This is the generation of them that seek him, that seek thy face, O Jacob. Selah.

7 Lift up your heads, O ye gates; and be ye lift up, ye everlasting doors; and the King of glory shall come in.

8 Who is this King of glory? The Lord strong and mighty, the Lord mighty in battle.

9 Lift up your heads, O ye gates; even lift them up, ye everlasting doors; and the King of glory shall come in.

10 Who is this King of glory? The Lord of hosts, he is the King of glory. Selah.

~To the Reader~

Beloved,

Thank you for taking the time to allow me to share my story with you. I pray that this memoir will be a source of encouragement. Please know that no matter what you have gone through in life, you can trust that God will and can see you through. Trust your instincts and believe that you can make it. God has a plan for all of us. His plan is that we succeed and not fail. His plan is that we thrive.

With Love,

Lorraine

Acknowledgements

To my Husband Donnie Ray Wilkes, you are the best thing that has happened to me. Thank you for your patient love. To my son, Jeffrey Dont'e McKelvin, I love you with all my heart. To my four sisters of the same mother, Diane, Marsha, Cynthia, and Yvonne Jenkins, I dedicate this book to you because I love you all. We survived! Finally, to Aunt G, thank you for your strength and courage.

Contents

Introduction   1

Lorraine's Prayer   3

Glossary   4

Chapter 1   Vilma's Birth   5

Chapter 2   Crazy Mama   15

Chapter 3   Dumpster Search   25

Chapter 4   Little Feet Running   33

Chapter 5   The Rescue   39

Chapter 6   Big John   69

Chapter 7   Complex G   77

Chapter 8   Gone   83

Chapter 9   Behind the Curtain   87

Chapter 10   Gra Mother's House   101

Chapter 11   The Promise   111

Chapter 12   Mama Please   117

Chapter 13   Mercy Pool   125

Chapter 14   Summer   133

Chapter 15   My Father   139

Chapter 16   Waiting   149

Chapter 17   Fifteen   157

Chapter 18   Sweet Sixteen   161

Chapter 19   Last Year of School   169

Chapter 20   Graduation Day   175

Chapter 21   New Love   183

Chapter 22   Life Goes On   201

Chapter 23   Home   207

Chapter 24   Forever Home   211

Meet the Author   215

Introduction
"The Purpose"

The purpose of this book is to lead many out of their *F.O.G.* (*Fear of Greatness*), without shame of what has happened to them. Life will not be fair, and we will have trouble. There will even be events that may shake us to our core. From experiences, we know that life may not be all that we want it to be. In my memoir, you will see that abuse (sexual violence, physical, verbal and mental) can come from many sources such as grandparents, an aunt, spouses and sometimes children.

We may have deadly secrets from our past that we dare not share. Unfortunately, these secrets are still empowered to cause us shame, hurt and emotional destress. However, you must pay attention to the positive voice on the inside of you, which will tell you never give up.

Trust the inner voice that says to you, "You can make it. You are somebody." Trust God to help you to make it. Even if you feel that you may not know God, He knows you! Moreover, God will help you to make it through your situations.

The events may not have been good, but it will all work out for your good. You can be completely free of past hurts. You can move on into the future with great hope. No matter who told you that you do not matter, we all matter to God. We can and do survive. We can all find our *Forever Home*.

Solely, this book is written to remind you that you can make it, no matter what has happened to you in the past. You will survive and do not have to suffer in silence. There are many who have gone through domestic violence and survived. Moreover, as one of the many, I am coming forth for those who may have died in domestic violence or are still afraid to speak their truth!

Still, there are others enduring and striving to be accepted and free in their minds from tortures of being beaten, mishandled, overlooked, and rejected. As the voice of many who are afraid to be heard, I want to inspire and encourage that even when you do not know God, He is there in the darkest moments. He has given you life and loves you unconditionally, no matter what. Let go of the past and move forward.

Love Life Enough to Live.

Love Life Enough to Forgive.

Lorraine's Prayer

Dear Lord,

Bless those who read this book. I fervently pray that when this book is read, they will find the strength needed to survive and get out of whatever abusive situation he or she may find himself or herself in.

I command them to be free from guilt, shame, and pain. The past shall no longer plague their way of thinking. All things associated with a bad memory will be replaced with a good memory and a desire and will to have a healthy life will spring forth.

Help those Lord who are holding past hurts in their hearts. Help them to be free enough to talk about their situations and to release those hurts. I pray that they totally surrender to You and allow You to make them whole; in Jesus' name.

Amen!

Glossary

F.O.G. (f.o.g.): In this memoir, it is the acronym for Fear of Greatness

Fog: a thick cloud, something that obscures and confuses a situation or someone's' thought processes. To be bewildered or puzzled in a muddle, daze, or confused state.

Domestic Violence: Violent or aggressive, behavior within the home, typically involving the violent abuse of a spouse or a partner, let me add parental abuse from a mother, father, grandmother, or caretaker, child or sibling.

Rejection: dismissing or refusing a person's affections

Chapter 1

Vilma's Birth

I was born in Brooklyn, New York's Kings County Hospital in the year of 1958. This area is better known as Bedford Stuyvesant (Bed sty- do or die)! Even though I was living with Mama when I was born, I was named Vilma by my Aunt Gail, who was my great aunt, but my mother Charity's aunt.

Aunt G told me that my name came to her in a dream and Vilma Jenkins meant Determined Protector. I was always protecting everyone, so the name fit perfectly. Even at five years old, I knew that I was meant to take care of my sisters. People would often call me an old lady because of it. Nevertheless, everyone said that I was beautiful with my long, coarse hair. I was tall for my age with skinny legs; they said I had legs like John and my skin was caramel colored like his. What I did not like though was my skin. It looked like I had bumps on my face which my cousins from New Jersey would call speckles. My cousins would tease me and call me speckled face, which I hated. I also hated my skin because it looked like it was never clean because of all the marks on it. Aunt Gail said that when I was born, I was light-skinned, but as I got older, my skin tone turned darker.

People said that I was too good and wanted to be perfect, especially around Aunt G (Gail). My New Jersey cousins would visit and along with my sisters would call me "Goody two shoes" to tease me. Often, they would say, "She never does anything wrong."

Everyone said that I was Aunt G's favorite out of everyone else. They also said that it was rare for Aunt G to have a favorite anything or person. I felt special at times; I think I just felt important to have such an awesome task of being the keeper of the money. I liked it when people would ask, "Can you soften her up for us?"

Gail Jenkins was a strong-willed woman of good financial substance. I guess all the family assumed I was the favorite because she never fussed at me the way she would the other family members. I got my share even though she would speak to me in a softer tone. She told me often that I was smarter than the rest.

"You are smart; you have school smarts. But Vilma, you just do not have any common sense," she would always say. When she spoke to me, she never forgot however to talk about how bad my father was. She would say terrible things concerning my father.

"He is a no good man who did not want to take responsibility for his child. He did not want you!" It was easy for me to ignore her words. While she fussed, I just tuned her out. It was easy to put my mind on something else.

Most of the time she would treat me nice. I could get money when no one else could. The family would come to me when they wanted money from her and asked me to talk to her first.

But one day, Mama told Aunt G that my father refused to acknowledge that I was his child. He said that he was not going to give child support to a child that did not look like him. When Mama said that he denied I was his child, Aunt G became upset. Everyone whispered that I was her favorite person and that was why she was so upset.

My father was called Big John and all I ever heard was Big John, "No-good Big John." Aunt G described him as a tall, slim drink of water, with long skinny legs, handsome but a no-good dark complexion of a man. She said that he would not work anywhere. All he did was let women take care of him. I even heard that he dated many women from all different races.

Repeatedly, Aunt G would tell others and me how he disowned me at birth. "Big John had the nerve to tell me, "She does not look like me!"" She would go on with her drama. "He would ask, "Why is she so light-skinned?" Then she would walk away, showing whoever was still listening how he walked away. My Aunt G and Mama took him to court and Aunt G held me in her arms during the court proceedings.

She said that the judge ordered Big John to give Charity my mother eleven dollars a month for child support. Aunt G recounted her observations like this. "I told him right there in the court room to take that child support and stick it! I will take care of her and Charity as I have always done; even though she looks just like you, piece of black crap!"

Aunt G mocked my mother about how she just sat there in court, holding her head down like she always did. "Your own mother did not say a word in court to defend you or herself," Aunt G would continue to fuss about mama and Big John. After that she sent us back home to our small apartment in Brooklyn.

Aunt G often complained about how men talked to Mama when they were out together. She said they would say; "Look at that beautiful woman with her smooth colored caramel skin." I guess she looked like a yummy caramel apple to the men. The men love that slim waistline and big round hips which all the women in the Jenkins family had.

Never put on straight, Mama wore bright red lipstick on her full round lips. Her hair was shiny, black, thick and long and always out of place. She tried to comb her hair but never succeeded at getting it to look like it was combed. Her hair was messy and unruly like her. Her modest apparel dress hit right about her knees, but always discolored. She would wear the same outfit for days. Yet with all her messiness, the men loved to be in her presence.

When we would visit Aunt G, she would always look at me and say, "Unfortunate little thing will never amount to anything with all her brains. What good is being smart going to do her?" Even though I was just five years old, I understood the words never amounting to anything was not something good. I was told often that I was not worth much. Even as a small child, somehow deep inside of me, I hoped for more in life. I prayed that I would be able to do something special to help others.

Aunt G said that I was born to a crazy mother and a no-good father. When we went to Aunt G's house, I made sure not to speak at all. I stayed in the background in any situation. I would not talk at all unless someone was speaking to me. I had a lot to say in my head. If only they could hear what I was saying back to them. It would have made their heads spin.

I became a part of any wall in a room. I could listen to everything that was being said and no one knew that I was even in the room. I was bold enough to be in the room to listen to the conversation, but I was in constant fear of being noticed even though I wanted to hear what was being said. I took the risk just to hear. Whenever someone spoke or happen to notice me, all I heard was words of negativity and hate.

I longed for acceptance, just wanting to be noticed, loved and treated as if I was human. I wanted a mother and father who wanted and loved me. Fear was always gripping my mind. I was always fearful that I could do nothing right, fearful of being beaten or being sent away and the fear of rejection from those who were supposed to care for me. My reality was like a bad dream, so I daydreamed all day about the kind of life that I wanted.

The *fog* was very thick in my mind; I could not see reality, nor did I want to see reality. I would act as if I did not care about anything or anybody. Often people called me a strange child and said that I seemed old for five years old. I would laugh at whatever was said to me because it kept me sane. When something happened, I would just laugh.

Living with Mama was not easy; I had to fend for my two sisters and myself. She would leave De-De, Margaret and I often. De-De was a spunky little thing at four years old, very lively, and happy all the time. Nevertheless, at four years old, she would speak her mind. She would tell anybody what she was thinking and what she thought about them. She was fair skinned and petite; Mama seemed to love her the most. Mama would cuddle up to her, smile and tell her how much she loved her little baby.

At three years old, Margaret was darker skinned and quiet. However, she would get loud when having fun. Margaret could stay by herself all day and have fun without speaking to anyone. I oversaw all the household duties as much as one could at the age of five. I tried to make sure that the girls got dressed in the morning and all their basic needs were taken care of.

I always felt like I was having an out-of-body experience. I was floating through the fog of life. I felt like I was writing a story in my head as I was moving through it and I was on the outside looking in on a story that seemed unreal to me. There were times life would become so painful and unbearable that I would zone out in order not to feel. I was not allowed to feel or express my feelings, especially as a child. We were not to express anything to adults. Whenever I tried to talk to Mama, she would say, "Just shut up and don't say a word!" Therefore, I would keep everything inside. I would talk to myself in my head, while trying to figure out the world and plan my future. I would fantasize for hours about a better day.

I stayed numb to what was going on around me. I would act like what I saw or felt was not real. Yet there were voices in my head talking to me about what I was seeing. I saw life through a thick fog of smoke. I felt like I was walking through the street on foggy day, unable to see. During my foggy days, I could still function, but I had to be careful not to walk into walls and I was careful not to walk into an unpleasant situation.

I did not want to walk into Aunt G or Mama; Aunt G was always screaming at Mama. I felt like I was in a bad story or movie. Things were not good, yet somehow my sisters and I found laughter in every situation all the time.

Laughter was our way out. We laughed about everything and everybody. If something bad happened, we laughed. If someone looked funny to us, we laughed. We would even look at each other and laugh. Laughter was used as our secret language for "Look at that" or "Be careful." The family members would make comments concerning our laughter; they would say those silly girls laugh all the time. They did not understand that laughter was the method we used to throw people off from thinking that they were hurting us. The laughter ensured that we did not take in all of the hurtful comments as personal.

I did not understand why I was here on this earth. I did not understand why I was born into the environment I was in. I did not understand what was going on around me or in my mind.

I tried to avoid conflict at any cost. When we were at Aunt G's house, our best bet was to stay out of her way, or she would make us regret being in her path. She would embarrass you with her words or take a stick and swing it at you, and she did not miss swinging that stick.

I managed to get away from her when she was in a bad mood. I could ignore her most of the time; I would just go somewhere else in my mind. I would not respond to her threats or demeaning comments. If I found that I needed to respond, I would do so in my mind.

My sister De-De seemed to always be in Aunt G's line of fire. She could not stand De-De. Honestly, I believe she hated her due to her skin color, which was a light porcelain color. She was prejudice against her own great-niece. De-De was beautiful; her skin looked like it glowed and was flawless. Aunt G was so jealous of that.

When De-De got close to Aunt G, she would call her some awful names. "Get out of my face you good for nothing half-bred Spagnola! Who is your daddy? Do you know? Of course not! Some drunk Spagnola is your daddy but no one knows who. I can't stand yella people; they think that they are better than everyone else because they are lighter than the rest of us."

As young as De-De was at the age of four, she would talk back. "Mama knows who my daddy is." I tried to protect De-De from her. For whatever reason, De-De would try to get close to her; she would try to get Aunt G's attention by arguing back at her.

There were times that she would try to get Aunt G to like her. She would even try to make conversation with her. Aunt G would just carry on with the insults. "You will never know who he is. You will never amount to anything ever. Your daddy is some drunk your crazy mother met in the street and had sex with. Get away from me before I hurt you! Move now; I can't stand to look at you!" De-de would stand there bold and defiant looking at Aunt G in her face until Aunt G would knock her little body to the floor. Aunt G would step over her, and keep on walking past her, cursing at De-De.

I tried to the best of my ability to divert the attention away for De-De. I would tell her that I washed the clothes or cleaned up her room for her, hoping it would please her. But that just a far-fetched fantasy.

Chapter 2

Crazy Mama

Charity Jenkins was my mother. I have no real background information on her. I do not even know when her real birthday was. I heard she was born in South Carolina, but the family moved to New York. No one in my family talked openly about the family's background. Everything and everyone was a secret.

All I know for sure is that my mother was crazy. There were many conversations about Mama concerning her strange behavior and her strange illness. Mama would walk around the street talking to herself and listening to the voices she said were in her head. She would ask, "Do you see them? Can you hear them?" I would try to listen for the voices, but I heard nothing. With everything within me, I wanted to hear the voices with her. I wanted to understand what she was seeing and going through. I wanted to live in her world.

Aunt G said that she would be sick for days and the doctors could not figure out what was wrong with her. Between her hearing the voices and getting physically sick, no one could explain what was wrong, but our cousins said that she was acting crazy. They also whispered somebody "put roots" on her.

I asked Aunt G what were "roots." To my surprise, she answered my question with a serious look on her face. "Roots is a spell cast from our ancestors." Aunt G said she would go to the root lady. "I take her some money. She gives me advice on how to take care of my enemies; she tells me what to do to destroy them."

She said that the Root woman gave her powder and spells to change things. She said that she could put roots on people to make them do what she wanted them to do. "I can get them off my back if they are troubling me," she said. She said that you put the potion in their food or drinks. You could even put the powder on a lover's pillow to make him act the way you wanted.

I overheard some of the relatives talking, that Aunt G took Mama to the Root woman one day and she had put some roots on her. After she left the Root woman, she was acting crazier; talking to herself more and more, running around the streets, and going wild like an animal. Why would Aunt G do that to my mama I wondered?

Aunt G took me along with her to the Root Lady's house one day. As I was walking up to the door, I walked into an awful smell. It smelled like ammonia and strong chemicals mixed together. The smell hit my nostrils and made my head spin. I began to visualize that I was in a dark room and laying in a coffin. As we walked through the doors together, she told me to sit down in the foyer.

While sitting in the dark, damp room of the foyer, my head started feeling clearer. I looked around the room and saw black curtains covering the walls. The curtains look like they have been on the wall since the beginning of time; they were dark, dusty with an odd hospital smell.

There were other people sitting around in the waiting area. These people looked sad and almost like ghosts. No one spoke to anyone else or smiled. After a while, Aunt G came from the back holding a brown paper bag tight in her hands. With a weird smile on her face, she told me to come on because she was finished and ready to go. As we left, she mumbled to herself, *"I will fix them. She should have left that man. He was married to another woman; he should have told her that he was married. Now somebody put the roots on her. I know for sure now that lady told me the whole story. They took her mind straight from her."* The family whispered that she had lost her mind because of my father, Big John. But then again, how could someone take Mama's mind? I was so confused.

Aunt G continue to talk to herself. *"She fell in love with Big John. That man does not love her; he wants every woman that he sees. Any man who has so many women in his life is no good."* Stories were told of him that he loved all woman, no certain type; Indian, Spanish, black, white and they all loved him back. Aunt G went on and on about Big John.

I continued to wonder in my mind. Was the trip to the Root lady about him? Aunt G went on to talk about how he looked. *"Tall black drink of water. Wearing that beard trimmed to perfection with his smooth dark skin, long lean skinny legs, and his slim built body. Cool whisper that he would speak in. The women are stupid,"* she would say on our way home.

I thought now, "Who is talking to herself?"

"He is too good at convincing women that he loved them. He was not happy with one woman; he had to have at least two. He messed with the wrong one this time," she murmured. My father did not stay with any woman long. He would get bored and soon leave the nest that he and the woman made together, leaving her to take care of the home by herself. He would soon find a new home and new woman to take care of him. I would get tired of Aunt G talking about my father and would just pray to get away from her.

The stories were numerous about what made Charity my mother sick in her mind. I heard one of the relatives argue saying, "You are all wrong! Charity is sick because of the abuse she encountered due to her mother abusing her. She started hurting that child when she was a baby at six months old. Charity is unable to function day to day as a mother due to her trauma. Her mother hated her. I have never seen such hatred toward a baby before in my life!" The cousin exclaimed.

Mama was unable to care for us, as a mother should. I would stare at her trying to figure her out. She would catch me staring and stare back without saying a word. Her stare would send chills up and down my spine; I would just walk away with an uneasy feeling. I often wondered why she did not love me and because of the disconnection between us, it wounded me in my heart. Mama did not say much to me; she was cold towards me, even in the tone of her voice. If I tried to get close to her, she would say, "Get away from me." She looked at me as if it was painful for her to see me.

Mama did not smile often. Whenever she was excited enough to smile, her bright teeth would show and her whole face would light up. It was such a wide unexpected large grin on a small framed face. Her large wide grin would lighten up the room and made me smile on the inside as well. When she had her moments of being loving and warm towards my sisters, she would read the Bible to us on some of the nights she was home. We would all pile up together in one bed. Mama would get the big Bible with the picture of the white man with the long hair on it and she would read to us. I remember she would say, "We are all that we have. You all must take care of and love each other no matter what. People will try to separate you. Do not let them separate you; stay together." She would take strands of our hair and put it in that big old Bible. Those were loving feelings and good memories for my sisters and me.

However, on her bad days, which seemed to happen more than the good, Mama would get a bewildered look on her face as if she was in mental anguish or physical pain. She had an expression on her face as if she wanted to scream but could not. She would hold her head in her hands and shake her head hard. When she started acting like that and got that look on her face, I knew that it was time for her to go out. I could almost tell when it was time for her to leave us. I always wanted to know where she went and what she was doing in all that time she was not with us.

Mama would leave my two sisters and me for days at a time. I was six years old, De-De was four and Margaret was three. We were always hungry; I did not know what a full stomach felt like. My stomach would hurt and have cramps with air bubbles awful feeling. There was hardly ever any food in the house for us to eat due to an empty refrigerator. The house had very little furniture with one bed and an old wooden table with four chairs. I knew in my heart that things were not right. I knew that we should not have been living that way.

Whenever Mama was leaving us, she would shout back at me with a demanding voice, "Watch them! I will be right back." Mama's words would continue ringing in my ear, while I wondered why she was in such a hurry to get out of the house.

We were fearful at lot of the time. I never knew what to expect next. We were always in survival mode, searching in dumpsters for our next meal. Fear gripped my mind whenever Mama would leave us. I did not know who would show up at the door when mama was not home. She would tell us not to answer the door if anyone knocked.

Only Aunt G would show up sometimes. Moreover, we had better open that door when Aunt G knocked. Mama would tell us not to let Aunt G know she was gone but Aunt G could see that she was not there when she came into the house. Thankfully, when she came over, she would bring some food with her.

As I remember looking at my sisters' sad faces on the nights when we did not have any food, I felt bad that I could not do anything to help. All I remember thinking was we need food. On those nights, we went to bed hungry and I would wake up the next day thinking about how hungry we were and how to get food for us.

One morning, I remembered the night before listening for the latch to click as Mama walked out of our big brown door. Once

I heard the click behind her, I knew she would not be back for a while. I looked at the big door, which was the tallest door I have ever seen. *Click, click, click!* The sound seemed to linger in my mind from the night before. The sound of the latch clicking signified loneliness and that we were alone. Many times, when she left the apartment I would watch the door with great anxiety until I got tired of looking at it.

I would try to stay awake and wait for Mama to come home. While she was gone, I was afraid that monsters would come and get us. Mama was always talking to the monsters telling them to go away. I hoped that the monsters would not come and make us act like Mama did. As hard as I tried to stay awake, I would always fall asleep

This time she was gone for two days. What were we going to do? We had to fend for ourselves. We lived in a small apartment, in Brooklyn, New York. It was a quiet neighborhood compared to most of the area. I never heard much noise, or I did not pay attention to the noise. I was busy trying to make sure no one heard us. I did not pay much attention to the outside world.

There was nothing, but fear associated with going outside. Mama would say that there is nothing out there but bad people. *"Stay in here I do not want the bad people to know about you."* She said it was better if we stayed inside. She would promise to bring us something back good. She would say, *"When I get back, we are going to have fun. I will bring new dresses and pretty shoes."* She would promise to take us with her next time, so we could have an enjoyable time. *"What do you want to eat? French fries and hamburgers?"* I believed her each time she said that she would come back with all the food we could eat. I even pictured my new dress and shoes in my mind. I stayed up each night until I would fall asleep waiting for her with anticipation of the food and new clothes. We never receive that new dress or shoes from her. We did not get the French fries or that hamburger either.

Chapter 3
Dumpster Search

We were hungry at daybreak because once again, we went to bed the night before without eating. The girls were not making much noise that day and there was an eerie feeling in the house. However, my mind was focused on what could I do to get us some food.

I took my small frail six-year-old body and drug a chair from the dining room to the food cabinets. I struggled to climb onto the chair, searching with great anticipation about what I would find to eat in those cabinets. When I first peeked in, I did not see any food. I searched in all the corners of the cabinet; I refused to give up. I was nearly climbing into the cabinet, looking all around inside. Yet, I did not see any food.

Tears began to roll down my little face, snot running from nose, while I held my head down sobbing aloud. My stomach was hurting. I looked up again through my tears only to see a half bag of sugar, a can of pepper and a loaf of bread in the bare cabinet. Little De-De and Margaret hear me shoveling around in the kitchen and they came running to the kitchen table. "It's time to eat," I said with excitement. They smiled and quickly sat down. I got the bread down first from the cabinet to make sandwiches. I turned my back to them as I sprinkled water on the sugar to make a paste. Then I shook some pepper onto it. There were just a few slices of bread, enough for one slice of bread for each of us. I spread the sugar, pepper paste on one slice of bread, and folded it in half. I gave De-De one-half and Margaret the other half.

We ate those sandwiches as if it was the best meal we ever had. As I held my wet sugary, pepper sandwich, the soaked mixture of bread fell apart, as the water and sugar mixture slowly rolled down my fingers. I took my tongue and licked the sugary mixture before it would hit the floor. The sugary crunchy taste hit my tongue, sending a great sensation of pleasure to my body. What a great taste of good sugar melting in my mouth! After eating our meal, we went to sleep.

Our Mama was strange, always talking to herself and always asking for help aloud to people I never saw. She would tell us about the fun times she had when she was out in the street. She would say, "You should have been there, but no it's not safe for you outside these doors. I was having a fun time with men, partying and drinking at Ralph Avenue Park." I often wondered if she thought about us and tried to figure out why she did not want to be with her children.

In the 1960's, Ralph Avenue Park in Brooklyn, New York was a place where "colored" people went to dance, play music, drink, and make out. No one outside of the neighborhood would dare go to this park. The police did not go to the park, for fear that, the colored people would hurt them or that they would have to kill someone. The police did not care what the colored people did to each other in this park. Therefore, the park was a place of freedom for colored people. The music would be loud along with the drinking and talking, but fights would break out at a moment's notice. When fights broke out the people would run as fast as they could. Mama had us there one night when we had to run. Even dead bodies were found there, but that did not stop the people or Mama from going there.

People and Mama went to the park to escape their problems. I believed Mama's problems were us, her children. She said we could dance all night long if we wanted to. She loved to dance and felt free when dancing outside in the air. People talked about Mama being in the street. Stories would flood the neighborhood on how they would see her get in strange men cars and leave with them for days at a time.

I was happy when Mama on occasion returned home with food and money for us though. Mama would place the food on the table and without even looking directly at me, she would bluntly say, "Feed them." When she did look at us, it was a blank look with no feelings. It seemed she would just look through us, as if we were invisible. I do not know if she saw us or not, but I felt like she did not see us.

She had a special strange liking for De-De more than Margaret and me. She called her Little Pussy Cat. De-De was a chubby pretty little girl, light-skinned and five years old at the time. It was rumored that she was Puerto Rican; I guess because of her complexion and features. She would hug and kiss on De-de all the time. Always carefully handling her, she would treat her tender like she was going to break. She would say, "Make sure she does not get hurt; she is my baby."

I often wondered what Mama looked for outside our home. Did we matter at all? What was more important than us — her children? Did Mama care that her children were hungry? Did she understand that we struggled to eat? I never bothered to tell her about the sugar sandwiches I had to make for us. As our mother, she should have known. Meal times were times of worry, even though most of our days were spent jumping around, playing and laughing. But when it was time for us to eat, I had to fix what I could find.

Once a week, Mama would take us out with her. And on this particular night, she was excited and happy. As she put on her make up with her red lipstick, she instructed me to get the girls

28

ready because she was taking us out for a walk. I jumped up and down, happy as I could be. She was taking us out with her! As we were on our way out the door, I saw a big yellow stop sign on our door with the word "Eviction" on it. I had not seen a sign on our door before, so I wondered what it meant? But I did not give it any more thought.

It was dark outside, and the girls were quiet. They were always afraid of the dark. They held tight onto my hands; all of us not knowing what to expect. We walked with Mama for what seemed like hours. My feet were hurting, and I was hungry since we had not eaten all day. We finally stopped in the park and sat by some big black steel dumpsters. As we sat down, we frowned our faces at the smell of the garbage coming out of that large can. Even though the can was taller and bigger than we were, the stench easily made its way to our noses.

Mama pointed her finger at the can and smiled. "There is some tasty food in the can for you all," she proudly said. Then to my surprise, she reached out her arms and picked me up. Sadly, I felt strange being picked up by her because she never reached for me. In my mind, I was thinking that she was about to throw me into that big dumpster. Afraid, I started squirming to get away from her.

"Hold on before you fall," Mama said. "Climb up," she hissed as she held me up to the dumpster. I was thinking, *"This is a garbage can. How are we going to get food from here?"* I shut my eyes tight and did not want to do this. She was holding me like one would hold a feisty cat. I had never been allowed to touch her, so I was not going to hold onto her or touch her for that matter. Scared of what she might do next, I peeked my little head into the can. Thinking it was dark and stinky, I was sick to my stomach, feeling like I would throw up. she said that there was food in the can for us to eat.

Still at my young age of six, I understood that we needed to eat to survive. I found the strength to open my eyes and calm down my stomach. As I proceeded to look around the dumpster to find food I heard my mother say, "If you want to eat, search around!"

Therefore, I put my small hands in the garbage and swished around. I tried to do it quickly because it was pitch black in that bin. Terrifying thoughts for a six-year old ran through my mind. *What if there are rats in here and I fall into this garbage can?* My heart was pounding fast in my chest, but I managed to put away my fear and continue to search. I knew the girls needed to eat and so did I. I could not see very well inside the dumpster, so I just grabbed at anything that I could reach. I grabbed a sandwich and several containers with drink left in them. I even pulled a sandwich out, which had some dirt on it. I tried to clean it off and brushed off anything else that did not look good. I tried to pass the good parts to the girls.

Surprisingly, they did not seem to care that we were eating from this dumpster. Hunger had numbed their senses of smell and taste. I continued to search for more food and found some half-eaten chicken and bitten off burgers in the dumpster. Somehow, I did not smell the stench anymore. I was focused on eating and making sure the girls had food. I found more drinks for us and we ravenously ate and drank what others deemed as trash. My sisters literally grabbed the food from my hands without complaining or thinking about it came out of the garbage. In our minds, the food had been washed just for us to eat. We ate until we were full and fell asleep on the bench.

Shortly, Mama woke us up out of our sleep, but I was still tired. It was still dark and quiet outside. The streetlights provided little illumination, but Mama said that it was time for us to move on. She started walking ahead of us; I followed her, and the girls held onto me as we walked. I held onto them as well as to protect them. I always watched out for the girls; they were afraid and so was I. I could see the fear on their faces, but I could not show my fear. It would only have scared them more.

As we walked, I looked around for monsters or someone to jump out and get us. I believe we walked for an hour. I was so tired; I just wanted to sit on the ground. The girls complained, asking if we could stop because they were tired. "Be quiet," I whispered. "We will stop soon to rest." My words calmed them for a while. Then I sang made-up songs to them as we walked. *"One day we are going to play all day long and eat all the ice cream and cake we want."* They joined in the tune and Margaret started humming, "Yum, yum, yum." We laughed, kept walking and hummed the made-up tune. I would always make up songs to sing and they would just go along with it. On the other hand, I would try to say something funny and they would forget they were scared and start laughing.

We loved laughing and playing our made-up games. During all of that, it helped us to forget, at least for a brief time, the problems we had just to survive. We could forget the loneliness and the hunger by just laughing for a little while. Laughing seemed to take the sting out of our troubles.

My sisters would roll around the floor and laugh until they could not breathe. Then I would start laughing until tears would come out of my eyes and I could not breathe. My stomach would be hurting when I finally stopped laughing. However, we would look at each other and laugh all over again. It is amazing how the mind and body discover coping mechanisms when pushed to their limits.

Chapter 4
Little Feet Running

*M*ama looked over at us and pointed to a big white car, "Get in," she said as she put her finger over her lips signifying do not speak. I climbed in first; the girls follow. As I got in with hesitation, I noticed that the car smelled good. The big car was all white even on the inside. It was a little cold outside, so it felt good to get into the warm car. We curled up together in the back seat and held each other. I do not know or remember if Mama told us to go to sleep, but I thought I heard those words as I drifted off. As I was falling asleep, I did hear her say in a soft voice that it was warm and cozy inside of the car.

Suddenly, I was awakened to someone screaming at us. There was a man inside of the car with us! "What are you doing? Get out of my damn car before I call the police!" He screamed. "Get out; get out of here right now! You bums get on my nerves!"

My heart was beating so fast. It felt like it was about to come out of my chest. I pushed the girls out of the strange man's car and we scatter to get out of the big white car. Our little feet ran as fast as they would go. I looked back, and Mama was standing outside of the car, but she did not appear as afraid as we were.

She did motion us to run. Therefore, we did, and Mama followed us.

After our escape, we walked until daylight, finally arriving home. Mama did not say a word about what happened. Instead, we all crawled in bed together and slept. Mama did sleep with us sometimes when she was home. Those were considered happy times when she would curl up with us in the bed.

Nevertheless, on this occasion, I was awakened by her laughing loudly to herself. I thought, *who is she laughing at* since there was nobody in the room but her. There were moments she would laugh at something or someone that we could not see. When she laughed, it seemed like the whole room would light up; however, I was trying to figure out what was so funny to her that particular day. I looked at her great big, wide grin, which seemed to go from ear to ear.

I remember feeling good because Mama was happy, but then I got sad at watching my mother go through her different emotions. Laughing one minute and screaming out for help the next. I felt sad when she was laughing, because it seemed to be triggered by some imaginary person she was seeing. Her facial expressions were as if she was laughing and crying at the same time. I wanted to laugh with her, but I did not know why she was laughing. It made me a little scared to see her like that and afraid to join in the laughter with her.

Even though our mother stayed away from home a lot, having my sisters made it easier and less frightening. We held tightly on to each other and kept each other company. We did not have toys, so we used each other as a toy. Oftentimes, we passed the time with our made-up games. Playing tag and running around the house were our favorite pastimes. We would run around the house all day, laughing, and screaming all we wanted to. No one ever told us to stop the noise because we were the only ones there.

Sometimes we were afraid, but that emotion did not last for long. Soon we would forget and continue to play our games. There were times when we would laugh all day at anything and everything was funny to us. We loved looking out the window at the people passing by to make fun of them. We would laugh at how they walked or what they were wearing. We just did whatever we could to amuse each other.

As a child, I still wanted to go out with Mama even though we would at times end up in strangers' cars. I was eager to go whenever she would take us with her. Because at least we were with our mother and would not be alone. We still felt safer with her than without her. Being with Mama meant that we would not have to wonder if she would return because we would be with her.

Often Mama would tell me that we were about to go out again. She would allow us to go with her until she would have something else better to do. If we happened to with her, then at that point, we would have to go back home. I did not know what she had to do, but she would be in such a hurry to get away. I remember one instance we were on our way to find food. We were doing what we normally did, holding hands, making sure that we stayed close together. It was a very bright sunny day. When we walked outside, the sun felt warm on my skin. We were happy to be going out with Mama to hunt for food, which had become a normal thing for us. As I mentioned in an earlier chapter, I was in a daydream; I was in my *fog*.

When we were in the house, we could not see the sun and the house always seemed dark. Therefore, I thought it was dark outside, but of course, I was wrong. We never had sunlight inside the house, so I did not know any better. On that day, it looked like Mama had opened the shades to let the sunshine in; there was something different going on. Moreover, I felt like something was about to happen. My intuition and senses were on high alert, and even as a six-year-old child, I knew something was different about the day.

On this particularly strange day, Mama did not want me to get the girls dressed. She took her time and dressed us herself. She made sure our little dresses were clean and she combed our hair. I do not remember too many times that she would dress us; normally she would tell me to get the girls ready. If we were going with her, she did care what we wore. I was thinking that we must have been going to a special place to find food today. I got even more excited as she dressed and prepared us.

There was no food in the cabinets or in the refrigerator, not even sugar this time; therefore, I was happy about going out. Finally, Mama got us dressed. Then, she lined us up by age and looked us over; I was first, De-De second and then Margaret. She said, "You all look good enough now. Let's go!" As we walked outside into the sunlight, I held Mama's hand tightly. De-De held mine and Margaret held De-De's hand.

As I looked up, the sun blinded my eyes, but I saw a shadow of someone coming toward us. She looked strangely familiar; I had seen her before. The woman had a very serious look on her face, as she walked quickly towards us on her short legs. Since the sun was shining behind her, I thought I saw a halo on her head.

Normally I could ignore people I saw coming toward us. I would hold my head down; we were not to attract attention when walking. Mama would warn us not to look at anyone. "Just keep your heads down and keep walking fast," she would say. Again, I did not recognize the woman at first because the glare from the sun was shining bright in my eyes. However, as she got closer to us, I saw that it was Aunt G!

We were always happy to see Aunt G. Even though she did not smile, she always had something special for us. Immediately, I looked at the brown bag she held in her hand. It meant that it was for us. She would give us food every time she would visit. She would have sandwiches wrapped in plastic and I loved her sandwiches. She would make us tuna or shrimp salad sandwiches with lots of mayonnaise. Aunt G always gave us money for candy, but Mama would take it as soon as Aunt G would leave. I liked it better when she brought the candy herself.

Although I was glad to see Aunt G, I put my mind back on Mama. I stared at Mama and wondered where we were going and why we were dressed up. Whenever we were out with Mama, we could expect an adventure of walking and searching for food. Whether we were searching for that special garbage can where the food might be safe enough to eat or sitting and sleeping on park benches. I never felt safe even though she would try to reassure us that we were fine. When we were not with her, I wondered what she was doing while she was out. Furthermore, I often wondered if she thought about us being home alone.

Chapter 5

The Rescue

Aunt G was around thirty years old and stood four feet nine inches in height. She had a small waistline that showed off her large round hips. Her beautiful long, black thick hair was usually pinned up in a bun. However, her full round lips were usually dry and matched her dull dry skin.

There were no flaws in her skin besides the dull color. Actually, she was beautiful to look at. When she was dressed in her best gowns, she looked like a movie star. Her brown piercing eyes would just cut through you when she would give you that serious "Aunt G" look.

Gail Jenkins was her name, but Aunt G is what everyone called her. She was my grandmother's sister, my mother's aunt, and our great- aunt. Aunt G could swear like a sailor and drink rum with the best of them when the moment was right. At the same time, she was a smooth-talking Eastern Star Leader. She would dress in her furs and jewelry and behave like a queen in charge.

She was once married to a man we did not know much about and their union conceived two girls. One girl she treated like a queen who was light-skinned and the other girl who was dark-skinned, she treated like dirt.

All we ever heard was that her husband was no good and he cheated on her. She would talk about how he left her when she became ill with polio. Her disappointing marriage caused her not only to hate her husband, but also to hate all men. I heard that her husband was a dark as night and looked like the daughter she treated badly.

Aunt G had a nice side that most people did not see. She did not want anyone to think that she was nice; she was afraid of being taken advantage of. Therefore, she worked hard at hiding her heart of gold. She would give you the shirt off her back, but that shirt would cost you something later.

She was considered the "Black Queen" of the neighborhood. She was the only black person in the neighborhood who owned property and was the superintendent of the building that she owned. She also worked two other jobs, to make sure she did not lose her house. One job was in a big hotel in Manhattan called the Waldorf Astoria; one of the biggest hotels in the United States, as she would brag. Her other job was taking care of some white people's houses, by cleaning for them.

Everyone considered Aunt G rich in the neighborhood. She loaned money to a lot of people. Whenever someone needed money they went to Aunt G. Not only did they think that she was rich, they also thought she was crazy. She would be out on her stoop with her nightdress on, cursing at people for no reason at all. She also threatened those who did not agree with her. This petite woman would fight at the drop of a hat. Few people would challenge her authority when she talked. I believe they listened out of fear.

Aunt G said that she made her mother a promise. She said, "My mother called me to her deathbed. I sat down on the bed and Mother said, 'Gail make me a promise. I want you to take care of Charity. Not only do I want you to take care of Charity but take care of any children that she will have. I must keep my promise to my Mother," she told us. That was the sole reason she would put up with Charity and her craziness.

I then turned my focus back on Aunt G. I tried not to look at her directly in her face as she walked toward us. I held my head down, but as hard as I tried, I could not keep it down. I was drawn into her frowned gaze because she looked as if she was angry. She was in a big hurry as her shorts legs moved fast toward us. I sensed the urgency in her walk as she approached us because the closer she got to us, the faster she stepped. Aunt G looked like she was ready for business. She was dressed in a pale white buttoned-down top. She had on a flared white and black checkered polyester skirt and wore low healed black work shoes.

I held on tighter to my sister's hand. When they felt my grip tighten, they grabbed my hand tighter as well. I could see the anger and concern in her facial expression. Her steps sounded like thunder to me, like the ground was shaking. I became unsteady on my feet and fear grasped my mind as she approached us.

The closer she got, the dizzier I got. I said to myself, *that lady must be mad at somebody. I hope she is not mad at me.* As she walked in our direction I realized something was about to happen. I did not know what to do, but I was glad Mama had my hand. All I could do was hold on tighter to Mama's hand for protection. Suddenly, Aunt G snatched my hand firmly from Mama's! She did not pull me away hard enough to hurt me; just enough to ensure she pulled me away from Mama's grip. "Give me these children!" she growled at Mama. *What was she doing? Help me Mama*! I screamed inside my head, but the words would not come out.

My mind was racing one hundred miles per hour, mainly with thoughts of fear. Mama did not say anything as Aunt G took my hand and my sisters moved closer to me for safety. Mama and Aunt G shared a brief glance. I understood that they knew what was going on; the eye contact without words were understood between the two of them. Then the unspoken words became loud to me; *we were going away!*

I was hoping Aunt G was not mad at me. When she reached for my hand, I did not know what to think or do. As Aunt G took us with her, Mama did not say anything, did not protest, nor did she follow us. She stood still in place in the middle of the road and watched as we were taken. Aunt G was in control; she did not say anything to us. She just took hold of our hands and we walked away.

What was going on? We were supposed to be on our way, to find food. She looked at us and said, "Come on." She looked at me to move first, so I started walking and the girls followed me. Mama saw the concern in our faces and finally said, "Go ahead with your Aunt G."

What did she mean go ahead? Go ahead to what; go where? My heart was pounding fast in my little chest because I did not know what to do. But I did know that we did not have a choice; we were to go with her. We were afraid, but we went. We took a short walk a few blocks away from where we lived. There were so many tall, stone-colored buildings all around us. We were unware of where we were headed to, nor did we know what was about to happen to us.

We finally arrived at the tall building where Aunt G lived. She was still holding my hand in a way that comforted me. At a big red stone door, she led us up five steps. My short legs climbed the stairs with caution. Then we walked up another flight of stairs to another door. When Aunt G opened the door for us, the first thing I saw was a small kitchen table and three chairs around the table in a very nice and clean kitchen.

I thought she had brought us there to eat at her nice kitchen table. My mind was on food, since we had not eaten that day. It was already the afternoon, and we had no breakfast or lunch. Instead, she took us to another room. This house was huge compared to where we lived. Room after room, we walked through. The house was still pretty; many different antiques in each room and fancy furniture too. I had not paid much attention to the furniture when I visited Aunt G in the past. I thought, *wow another room; big bed rooms, small bed rooms!*

Aunt G told us we would be staying with her for a while until, as Aunt G said, "Your crazy mother gets her life together." We continued our tour of Aunt G's house. "This is your room," she said pointing to the room my sisters and I would sleep in.

"My room?!" I shouted with excitement.

"No fool," she laughed. "All three of you."

"All three of us will share the same room and bed?" I asked out loud.

Aunt G responded, "You can sleep with me in my bed and you better stay still in the bed, so I can sleep. Come on; let me get you girls something to eat." Those were the words that I had been waiting to hear all day, *let's get something to eat.* I paid no attention to whatever else she had to say.

Mama left us without saying goodbye, as she always did. We stayed at Aunt G's, but mother returned months later. I was seven years old when Mama returned with a bundle in her arms, wrapped in a pink towel. Without words, Mama handed the bundle to me. I opened the blanket and saw pretty eyes peeping back at me. The small bundle made a connection with my eyes and our smiles joined. And then, Aunt G interrupted the connection.

Aunt G was upset again. She said, "I do not know what to say to you anymore. I do not know what to do to help you. When is this going to stop Charity? I cannot continue to take care of children that you bring home. Now, you have gone out and had another baby for me to take care of, another damn mouth that is hungry. You really need to get yourself together and get some help for your damaged brain. I am going to have you committed before something bad happens to you out in the street!"

While Aunt G released her fury, I took my baby sister out of the line of fire. I held my sister and smiled, asking her name. Aunt G snapped and said, "Her name is another mouth to feed!"

Mama responded, "Her name is Chie." I was happy to see Chie. She was someone else we could play with. I was seven, De-De six, Margaret five, and now Chie. But she was all mine.

The fussing continued with Aunt G, but Mama was quiet. She better not had answered her back. There was no telling what Aunt G would do to someone who would talk back to her. "I told you to stay away from Ray," she scolded Mama. "He is no good. What has he done for you except give you babies along with beating your dumb behind? You are stupid. Have you learned nothing except to go out and have baby after baby? What in the world is wrong with you? I am so sick and tired of this mess. I don't know what to do."

I don't know what good all that fussing did. Mama left again for another year and returned with another bundle in her arms. I knew what to expect now at eight years old. I ran to the door to get there before Aunt G saw the bundle. I was excited to see what I had this time. I already knew what to do and what the bundle meant.

I asked her name, and Mama said, "Shy." She handed her over to me and said, "She is yours. This is her bag with her bottle and diapers. I know you will take care of her." I looked at Shy and she looked back at me. Shy had such loving, sweet bright eyes. By the time I held my head up to say something to Mama, she was gone out of the door. I did not give her much thought after she left. I took Shy inside and gave her a bottle.

There were now five of us at this point. I was nine, De-de was seven Margaret age six, Chie age two and Shy one year old. Mama came back to Aunt G's and stayed for a few months. One night while we were in bed asleep, I was awakened by a lot of noise that was going on in the kitchen. Mama was begging someone to stop hitting her. She kept saying, "Please Ray; do not hit me again. I am sorry." I heard that name before one day when Aunt G was talking to someone in the kitchen. Aunt G said that Margaret, Chie, and Shy's Daddy was named Ray. I wondered if this was the same Ray I heard about.

I was in my bed, but I had to take a chance to see this Ray. I snuck out of my bed and walked as quietly as I could. I did not want the wood floor to squeak or I would be dead for sure. I peeped into the kitchen. I looked up from behind the wall to see a big, tall black man who seemed to fill the whole room as he walked from one side of the kitchen to the other. I lost my breath because it felt as if he took up all the space and air in the room. He was darker than the night-time and I could hardly see him in the dark room. Yet I could hear him yelling. He was trying hard to whisper, but I could hear the anger in his voice.

I do not know where I found the nerve to get closer, but I did. I wanted to hear and see what was going on in there. I got up to get closer, peeping from behind the door to see what they were doing. Then I saw him shake her. After he would shake her, he hit her in the face and on her shoulder. I cringed; it made my stomach nauseated to see her hurt and crying. I was afraid, and I did not know what to do. I wanted to move, but I could not move; my feet were stuck. My whole face got hot, felt like I was burning up with fever.

I heard him say, "I cannot support any more kids. I told you not to have anymore. I have too many now!" As I tip-toed closer toward them, I was stopped in my tracks by a loud sound, like something was cracking. Then I heard the impact of something smacked! I decided scared or not, I had to look to see what was going on in the kitchen. What was he doing to Mama? I was as quiet as I could be without being seen. I got close enough to see what was going on. What I saw scared me so badly I began to pee on myself. I could feel the water rolling down my legs, but I ignored the pee. Besides, I could not move; my legs were stiff as a board. I stood there hoping that I was invisible to them. I did not want that big man to hit me like he was hitting my mother. I prayed that he could not see me... *Please Lord, don't let him see me.*

I saw his big, long black arm come down to her little skinny face like a hammer and connect hard to her skin. Tears were rolling down her face. She tried not to cry aloud; there were moments when she would just moan in pain. I saw him take his big black fist hit her in her face again. Mama was crying as she tried to cover her face with her hands. I could feel the pain in my chest.

I was listening as they argued, and he hit her again and again. I jumped as each lick fell to her face. Every time he raised that huge fist, it landed on her face hard. *What would he do to me if he knew I was here also?* I covered my mouth and wiped the tears from my eyes. I started trying to walk backwards to get to my bed. I stayed very quiet so that he would not know that I was in the other room listening. I was afraid that if he saw me, he would beat me as well.

I could see bruises all over her face from where I was standing. She was crying and holding her hands up to her face to protect herself from being hit again. When he finished beating her in the kitchen he walked out and left her alone standing there and crying. She stood there for a while and continued to moan and groan throughout the night. Finally, I went back to bed.

Waking up early the next day, I wanted Mama to go around Aunt G. And when she did, it did not take long for Aunt G to see her face. "What happened to you?" She asked. Mama had to confess that Ray beat her up the night before. Aunt G waited for him to return. This was the first time I wanted to hear Aunt G curse. When Ray returned, she cursed at him and chased him away.

At that point, I wanted to tell Aunt G everything, especially what he had done to me at Christmas. I woke up early and heard them rustling around. Ray and Mama were putting presents under the tree. Ray saw me peeping from under the covers and when he did, he went to the kitchen to get the pepper can. He took some pepper and tossed some in my eyes. My eyes were burning like fire. I tried to rub the pepper out, but the more I rubbed, the more it burned. I cried and cried. Eventually, my tears cleared the pepper from my eyes and I was able to sleep. I never told Mama, so I don't believe she knew about it. The next day was Christmas and I knew I had a toy since I saw them placing the toys under the tree. I was the first one up and ran to the tree for my special gift. I looked directly at the tree and there were several gifts. I searched for my name on a present, but I did not see it. I walked around the tree, searched through the packages, and shook each one. I even got on my knees to find my gift. After an hour of searching, I figured Santa forgot about me. There was no gift under the tree for me. So, I believed I didn't deserve a gift. Santa took it because I was not sleep and saw them with the gifts the Christmas Eve. As the girls came out for their gifts, I did not mention what happened on the night before. But I wanted to tell Aunt G because she was the one who had probably bought me the gift!

Speaking of Aunt G... Aunt G had a revengeful reputation. Everyone in the neighborhood knew about her competency for hurting people who crossed her. If someone borrowed money from her and did not pay her back what they borrowed, she would tell everyone in the neighborhood so that no one else would lend that person money.

People in the neighborhood called her crazy. They were afraid of her going to the Root lady, who the neighbors thought had power to hurt them or make them sick. She would often warn people that she knew people in high places who would hurt them or their families at her command. She said that she knew how to do things to hurt people that they would never forget.

We had everything that we needed living with Aunt G and more. We dressed better than anyone in the neighborhood and we ate well. We never locked our doors; they were opened to anyone who was hungry. People walked in at any time and Aunt G would help them.

The other kids in the neighborhood loved to sit on her stoop just to tests her. It was kind of a game for them. They knew she did not like anyone sitting on her stoop, especially after she had cleaned it. When she saw them on her property, she would ask them three times to leave her stoop. I remember one incident when I was ten years old. She yelled out of her third story window, "I am warning you! If you do not leave my stoop by the time I count to three, I am going to throw something on you that you will never forget!" Everyone laughed, including me. I was sitting on the stoop with my friends laughing and talking loud, having an enjoyable time. After she made her threat, she left the window. Well, we continued to have fun, forgetting Aunt G's threat. All of a sudden, we saw what we thought was water come flying out of her window! She went to her kitchen, boiled hot water mixed with bleach and threw it from the 3rd floor window!

Boy, you could see us run fast as we could, trying to get away from that boiling hot water and bleach mixture! We still laughed as we ran. It did not matter to Aunt G that we were her nieces. We received the same warning and punishment. "You riff raffs keep thinking that I am playing with you! Do not say that I did not warn you all. Next time, you better move faster." From then on, I would watch for the signs when she would throw her mixture on us. I made sure I warned everyone first. "You better move; she is not playing!" I would tell them.

Aunt G with her petite body walked fast and hard. She was easy to recognize toting that big bottom which was the family inheritance. She wore her hair in a bun and always had on work clothes with old shoes she got from her employers at the hotel. Aunt G worked every day it seemed, hardly having a day off. She worked at Waldorf Astoria, a prominent hotel in Manhattan. This allowed her to bring home all sorts of good, yummy treats like cakes, pies, and chicken. There was also the weird stuff like fish heads, which she would make fish-head soup. Ugh! I would look inside the soup pot and see the fish heads swimming around. I refuse to eat it, but nobody would eat that fish-head soup except Aunt G. She would sit at the table and sip that soup like it was so good. She also brought home octopus, boiled it for my sisters and I to eat like it was something special for us. But again, none of us would eat those weird recipes.

In addition to working at the hotel, she cleaned white people houses three times a week. After having such long days, she would come home and work on the building she owned, which we lived in. Aunt G was the superintendent of her own building. It was a brownstone in Brooklyn, New York; Bedford Stuyvesant, a tough neighborhood in New York. It was rare in 1960's for a black person to own property such as what she had. Her being a black woman with real estate property was almost unheard of.

The apartment building had six level floors. Aunt G controlled every floor as well as the people who lived there. Most of the people were welfare recipients and did not work. Aunt G made it her purpose to remind them just how lazy and trifling they were too. She let them know that she owned the building and she controlled them, their money and everything in the building. To prove it to them, in the winter, she turned off the heat around 8:00PM declaring, "It's time for everyone to go to bed including the tenants!" Those cold winters were no fun. My sisters and I would wear as many clothes as possible to bed and huddle up close to each other to keep warm. The tenants complained but Aunt G did not care about their comfort. She cursed them saying, "This is my damn building! If you don't like it, leave!" Despite that hard-nosed personality, she helped many. If someone had a bill they could not pay, she paid it. If their children needed clothing, she provided. Her doors were open to hungry and helpless people. They came to our house day and night, looking for help and she would help them. People would say though beware of her doing you a favor. Aunt G would hold it against them later and remind them of what she had done to help them. Indebted to her, they knew that they better be ready to repay when she needed them to.

She had one male friend who we called Mr. Bae. He was a quiet soft-spoken, gentle man. I hardly ever heard him say anything except, "Yes G." It was rumored that Mr. Bae was a married man. He visited around about twice a week to fix things in the house. But we thought Mr. Bae was her special friend, except she did not treat him like he was special. She cursed him whenever she felt like it. If she did not like his handiwork, she cursed at him. He would look at her in a way that she knew he did not like her cursing him. But good ole Aunt G would sharply respond, "If you don't like it, get your ass out of here! I can always get someone else." He would not say a word. He just kept on working, looking like a lost puppy. The way he would look at her made my sisters and I laugh. He looked at my aunt like she was candy, or the best thing he had ever seen. Even though she abused him with words, Mr. Bae continued to make an appearance. He always looked like a puppy dog in love when it came to her. I often wondered why he stayed. I guess he was afraid of her as well. One day Mr. Bae stopped coming around and I wondered what happened to him. I overheard Aunt G telling someone that old Mr. Bae died. She just said it as a matter of fact, no emotion or sadness. *The old man just died.*

Not long after the death of Mr. Bae, Aunt G hired a superintendent and his name was Jimmy. I was not sure where she met him, but he looked homeless to me. Besides, it was not unusual for Aunt G to help homeless people. He appeared at the house one day and moved into the extra bedroom on the end of the hall. He provided labor in exchange for paying rent. He was a tall soft-spoken gentleman about 60 years old. He was the perfect type for Aunt G to manipulate. He stood six feet two, slim build, and no fat on his lean body. He looked like he had not eaten in a while. He was unshaven, and scruffy looking, but he was soft-spoken and kind.

It was obvious that he was an alcoholic, because he smelled like alcohol all the time. Whenever I would peep in his room, I would see a bottle of Bacardi rum and beer on top of his dresser. Jimmy would go on drinking binges and after he binged, he would sleep for about two days before he could function again. Aunt G would get upset with him, bang on his door cursing, trying to get him to wake up to do some work. I never saw Jimmy fix anything. There were times I saw Aunt G slip into Mr. Jimmy's room late at night and they would get drunk together. I dared not say anything because I did not want any trouble with my Aunt G.

Sometimes Aunt G cursed him, and they would go their separate ways for days. He stayed in his room without speaking to anyone. He shared the kitchen with us, and when he got hungry, he cooked lamb chops. He loved lamb chops and we certainly loved his lamb chops. He seasoned and floured them, prepped for a hot greased pan. My sisters and I would smell the aroma and at the sound of the sizzling meat, we would time it just right. As soon as they were golden brown, Mr. Jimmy would leave the kitchen. We'd run into the kitchen and take the lamb chops and eat them. Mr. Jimmy would go back to the kitchen and look in the pan. Hiding where he could not see us, we watched him, scratching his head and looking around the kitchen for the lamb chops. We could see the puzzled look on his face and laughed at him while we ate his food.

He would ask himself, "Where is my food?" This is where I would make my innocent appearance, making this statement, "You ate it." He was so drunk sometimes that he did not know whether he ate it or not. He would put another one in the black cast iron pan and we would eat that one too. We laughed so hard that our stomachs hurt. Mr. Jimmy eventually caught on. Angry, he chased us around the house. He was not fast enough to catch us, and we laughed at him while running from him. I liked Mr., Jimmy. He was fun when he was drinking. He would even give us money when he received his social security check.

Aunt G's daughter Cheryl met Jimmy and they seemed to like each other right away, even though they were years apart in age. There was a thirty-year age difference. Jimmy was around sixty and Cheryl thirty. They had a lot in common though when it came to drinking. We would see them hugged up and drinking together.

Cheryl lived in the bottom floor apartment. She was tall and slim, standing at 5'8"; beautiful and dark as the night. She wore her hair short and straightened, slicked down with grease. She loved to wear pants and neatly tucked in shirts. She laughed most of the time, loved telling jokes and partying. She had a lifestyle that was not favorable to her mother. She could do nothing right in Aunt G eyes. She could not get along with her mother and she was an alcoholic. She and Jimmy got along well, more like boyfriend and girlfriend, which upset Aunt G. I thought that Aunt G was jealous of Cheryl and Jimmy's relationship. Aunt G argued with Cheryl about them being together.

Cheryl's flirtatious behavior with men infuriated Aunt G. Cheryl had a lot of boyfriends; she attracted men like she was a magnet. She had five children and four had different fathers. Cheryl would get pregnant and claim that she did not know when she was pregnant. No one knew she was pregnant until it was time for her to deliver. She would go to the hospital and come back with a baby, just like my mother did. She carried her children in such a way that her stomach never got big. When she returned with her child, it would be a surprise to everyone.

Cheryl's children lived with her part time. It seemed like they were with us more than her. When Cheryl went on her drinking binges, they lasted for about three days. After drinking hard for those three days, she needed a day or two to recover from her hangover. During recovery, she did not want anyone around. She put everyone out of her apartment, including her children. She did not care to keep her lack of parenting skills a secret. I would hear her screaming, "Get out and go upstairs!" Her children would come running upstairs to be with us since we lived two flights up from them. My cousins were aged from ten to five-years-old. They would tell me, "We must stay with you for a while because Cheryl put us out." They did not call her Mama; they called her by her first name. She did not want to be called Mama because she said it made her too old. "I am never going to get old," she said often.

Most days, we had ten children in one apartment. So, Aunt G decided that we needed our own apartment. She wanted all the children in one place to keep an eye on us. We stayed one flight up from her and I was responsible for everyone's well-being. I was eleven years old then and I took full responsibility and charge of the apartment.

I remember Cheryl's last child was a boy named Little Ray-Ray. He was small and dark, six pounds at birth. One day, I was babysitting Ray-Ray because Cheryl was out partying for about three days. The little boy cried and cried, and I did not know how to get him to stop. Aunt G came up stairs, looked at him and took him to the hospital. The doctor said that he was going through DT's, delirium tremens. He was born an alcoholic since his mother drank when she carried him. He was going through the DT's as if he was trying to stop drinking, even though he did not make the choice to drink on his own. He was also malnourished, and I felt bad for him. Little Ray-Ray stayed in pain and cried constantly.

I loved my cousin Cheryl even with her unruly behavior of drinking and partying. She was nice to me most of the time. But she and Aunt G fought all the time, which caused Aunt G to go to the Root lady for help to deal with her. Even though Aunt G was powerful in everyone's eyes, she needed help sometimes too. I can recall nights when Aunt G would go in her room with a bottle of rum and just cry out loud. I knew at that point that she was human too and overwhelmed with life's responsibilities.

But when people visited her at home, she treated them badly by bringing up their past mistakes. She told them that they were good for nothing and would never amount to be anything. People hated visiting her but needed her and what she had. Only one person I knew visited Aunt G out of sincere kindness, Mitt our cousin. My aunt did not have any devoted friends who loved her. I would sit at the kitchen table with her sometimes and listen to her talk bad about people. I sat there just to keep her company. I was thankful when our sweet cousin Mitt visited from New Jersey.

Mitt was a gentle lady, with a beautiful smile. She was very nice to us. She treated us like we were real people and not throwaways. I believe Aunt G liked her as well. Mitt listened to Aunt G vent about her issues. She did not judge, just smiled. She was the one person besides myself who could calm Aunt G down just by being in her presence.

I believe cousin Mitt could calm anyone down with her warm voice and her great big smile. It soothed their soul and her words were always pleasant and positive. She would say to Aunt G, "G things are not as bad as they look. You will make it. G, you were built to survive. You are a strong woman. God made you strong G. Hold on." She went on to say, "G, look around at all that you have accomplished." While Mitt talked to Aunt G, I could feel my own soul calm down.

Mitt visited once a year and I loved her visits. I also loved when her children were with her. They would spend the weekend and we had a fun time laughing and playing. When it was time for bed, we would jump up and down on the bed and chairs. Aunt G would treat us good when they were around, so we loved seeing them. We could get away with making more noise when they were at the house.

Aunt G received governmental financial assistance for keeping my sisters and me, but I do not know how much. I do know that people commented that she only took us for the money that she received. Her response was she did not need the government's money. She had three jobs and owned her building. The check arrived on the first of each month. By the time I was twelve, Aunt G gave me money to go buy food and clothes for my sisters. I loved going to the market because I bought what I liked; all the sugary cereals I wanted. When I returned home, Aunt G complained, "You better not run out of food; you will be on your own." In addition to Aunt G giving me money, she had a habit of losing it. She thought however, someone was stealing her money. In fact, she would hide her money and couldn't remember the hiding places. I tried to help by reminding her because there were times she had my sisters and me up half the night trying to find her lost money. Most of the time, I found it balled up in a sock or bag in strange places; behind the dresser, in the bathroom, and on the top shelf of the closet. She got tired of the charades and made me "money captain." I hid her money until she was ready for it. I was excited to hide it for her; I was glad that she trusted me that much. She could see the happy expression on my face. She would look at me and say, "You love money like a cat loves fish. Get out of my face."

Aunt G was tough to get along with; most people in our family hated her. They hated her due to her speaking her mind. If she thought you were not doing things right, she told you. If you were not living up to your potential, she told you. If you were a drunk, she told you. She never held her tongue or how she felt about someone or their lifestyle. I believed the person who hated her the most was my grandmother. She gave Gra Mother advice she did not want or asked for; therefore, they argued frequently. "You are always telling people how to run their lives," Gra Mother would say. To add insult to injury, Aunt G would tell her how to handle us and our mother. She told her, "You need to take care of your own grandchildren. Why do you have me doing what you should be doing? Why don't you take responsibility for your life?"

There were times I thought she was right about what she said. She just did not put her words in the subtlest way. Her words did not soothe but felt like angry bite marks on your skin. She really gave good advice in a most unusual way. For example, she told others, "If you were not so lazy you could do better in life." In classic Aunt G language, she said, "If you get off your *ass* and work, you would not be hungry. Stop sleeping around with all those men and you might find a good man. Stop drinking so much before it kills you. Nobody is going to give you anything for free." She had a special saying that took me some time to understand. "You riff-raffs *(meaning good for nothing),* you wanna know something else? You all are some strange people." She told her daughter Cheryl, "You have a bad disease, called laziness. You can't do anything with lazy people except kill them, because they are good for nothing."

When Aunt G was not fussing trying to get everyone straight, she cooked. Aunt G was a good cook! One evening she cooked rice, collard greens and neck bones. I was enjoying sucking on my pork neck bone when suddenly we were interrupted by yelling in the hallway downstairs. I went to the entrance of the doorway and saw a man standing at the foot of the stairs. I could not make out what he looked like, but I sure could hear him. He was looking up from the stairs yelling, "I am going to take over this building! There are too many women in here trying to act like men. I am going to show you what a real man can do for you! Come down here before I come up to get you!" He demanded. "Give me the keys to this building you witch!" he laughed and snarled.

Aunt G ran to the hallway where the man was. I looked at Aunt G and she was not afraid at all. She looked like an Amazon woman from one of those comic strips. She screamed back at him, "You son of a bitch! Do not come any further or you will regret it for the rest of your no-good life!"

"Ha, ha, ha!" He laughed and took the threat as a joke. Loud and cynical, he screamed back, "You witch, I am on my way up these stairs to show you what a real man can do for you! Stay right there!"

Aunt G looked at me and said, "I will be right back."

What do you mean stay right there? I thought, *Do something!*

She went back into the kitchen to get something that she had cooking on the stove, and it was not food. I wondered to myself, *why is she worrying about what is on the stove? This man was about to hurt us!* She screamed while heading toward the kitchen. "I am going to pluck your frigging eye out yo head!"

She screamed, "Keep on running yo mouth! You son of a bitch! Come on!"

I looked back in the kitchen from the door way, and saw the pot boiling over with a white, foaming solution. The smell filled with very strong ammonia. It choked me and had me coughing.

Aunt G warned him again, "If you come any closer, you will be sorry." He did not believe her and started walking up the stairs. Petrified, I watched him. He continued to address all the women in the building. Walking and spewing his threats, "I am going to show you all what a real man is like including the little girls. I am taking over now."

Aunt G warned one more time. "Make one more step and I will blind you. When I am finished with you, your frigging eye is going to come out of your head." He laughed like a mad man and proceeded to walk toward her. Aunt G hurried to the kitchen, grabbed the big black pot with the smelly stuff. She returned to the top of the stairs with the big pot in her arms. She gave one last warning, "Take one more step and your damn eye is going to fall out of your head." He laughed and kept walking. When he walked up two steps, the smelly concoction that was in the pot came flying out as she slung it toward the man's face.

As the solution of what I found out later was hot lye stuck on the man's face, he screamed and squalled like a cat in pain. I stood at the top of the stairs in shock. I could not move; my eyes were popped wide open along with my mouth. I had never seen anything like that before. My eyes followed as I watched his right eye roll out of his head, down his cheek, his shirt and hit the floor! It was as if everything started moving in slow motion. Blood was everywhere as he shrieked and screamed like I had never heard before. He sounded exactly like a wounded animal needing to be put out of its misery.

As I stood in the doorway in terror, Aunt G was talking to me. I could see her mouth moving, but I could not hear any of her words. She snapped her fingers in my face and demanded that I get in the house. She said, "I am going to jail. Do you hear me? I am going to jail!" She shouted to get my attention. "Listen, I will be back in two hours."

Aunt G called the police. They arrived, looked at the man and called the ambulance. The police asked Aunt G what happened, and she responded, "I am not talking until I see my lawyer and the judge." The man was unable to talk; he had passed out from the pain. The police put handcuffs on her and took her away in a police car. Aunt G did not resist; she looked at me and smiled.

I went back into the house and found it strange that the girls were in the living room playing. I wondered if they had heard any of the noise that was going on. I did not bother to mention anything to them. I was afraid thinking, *what are we going to do? How will we eat?* I waited for Aunt G and remembered that she said she would be back in two hours. I started counting the minutes and then one hour, then two went by. What would happen if she did not return? But I still believed Aunt G when she that she would return. She had never lied to me. I do not know if it was two or three hours. It was not long before she showed up smiling. "See I told you, my people will not let me stay in jail. I gave the judge our signal and he let me go. Wow, I am going to sleep now." She laughed and went to bed. Once again, Aunt G was in charge!

Chapter 6
Big John

My parents met when Mama was eighteen years old. Mama had never had a boyfriend before him. My father was known as Big John and had a reputation in the neighborhood for dating more than one girl at a time. He was dating another woman when he met Mama, but he did not tell her that he was. He roamed from woman to woman, house to house. He had a way with women, I guess. I overheard women once say that he took their breath away, when he looked at them. Slim built dark skinned, he looked like a handsome black Clark Gable, the movie star. Big John was tall around six feet two inches. When he walked into a room his presence seemed to take up a lot of space.

He used his good looks to his advantage, persuading women to do whatever he wanted them to do. He could make them believe whatever he told them. Aunt G always said that the song "Papa was a rolling stone" really fit him. He rolled from one woman to the next. He had women all over Brooklyn New York, and he did not have a preference. He loved Black, White and Latino women; it did not matter to him. They were all the same. He did not have much respect for women because he was known for beating his women and talking to them like he owned them.

My Aunt G believed he loved them and hated them at the same time. She did not know why they continued to bother with him knowing that he would not treat them with respect. She declared, "I would not have his no-good tail. I would be the one woman that would beat him myself."

Most of the women knew about his reputation but they did not care. They just wanted to be able to say that they were with Big John. I often heard the story of my parent's whirlwind romance. Big John was walking down the street one day in Brooklyn when he spotted Mama. She was a petite, beautifully shaped woman with a small waist and a big bottom; not too big, just the way he liked it. Her long black hair just touched her shoulders. She wore a pencil tight black skirt and a white polyester blouse. Her tight blouse exposing just enough of her plump, firm young breast covered by glowing smooth caramel skin.

Big John's eyes drank her in and he let out a "wow." He thought to himself, what she was doing walking the streets alone and quickly struck up a conversation. "Hi, what is your name? Are you lost? If you are, I can help you find your way. If you need someone to rescue you, I am here." Mama looked at him smiled and did not answer. "My name is John; my friends call me Big John. You look thirsty. May I buy you a soda?"

He finally got a "yes" out of her, as she smiled a half grin, held her head to the side and peeped up at him. They walked to the corner store together. He purchased a grape soda and chips for her. He smiled at her and she smiled back. In those rare moments when my mother smiled, that smile would light up a room. Her smile went from one side of her face to another. She had a wide grin with white teeth. When she smiled back, he knew he had her. At that time my mother was living with her Aunt and my father started visiting her.

A relationship formed. He took her to different restaurants. She loved going out with him and eating. She was hungry most of the time, since her aunt did not feed her. Mama was feeling something good, something she could not describe. Aunt G took one look at Big John and asked Mama, "Where did you get this alley cat? An "alley cat" was a term Aunt G used to describe a man who did not have good character, did not work, nor had self-respect. "Send him back to the alley you got him from." Aunt G then looked at Big John and said, "You are not good, and you are up to no good. Get out of here and do not come back, you no-good riff raff!" Once again, she tore into my mother. "Wow, are you stupid? You can't see that he is no good? What is wrong with women today? You will just pick up anything and call it a man. Just because he is wearing britches does not make him a man."

A few months later Aunt G found out that Mama was pregnant with me and she cursed Big John when he came to visit. She said, "I knew that mother so and so was no good." But Mama would not hear it. Her response was, "We are engaged to get married and we are going to set a date. He told me that he loves me."

Aunt G heard *everything* Mama said and had a fit. She started throwing things around the house. Aunt G told Mama that Big John was going to leave her because she became pregnant by him. Eventually, Big John stopped coming to see Mama on a regular basis. So Aunt G had to find out what was going on with him and decided to investigate. She saw him in the street one day and followed him home. She saw him stop at a building only two blocks away from her apartment building. He was talking to a woman and he looked cozy with her. Aunt G asked the neighbors, "Who is that woman he is talking to? They easily replied "Oh, that's Gloria, his wife. They are having a baby."

The neighbor continued to volunteer information to Aunt G and said they got along most of the time. She said, "Big John stays out at night and the rumor is that he has another woman somewhere else. When he arrives home drunk, he wants to fight with his wife. I hear them arguing and fighting from my downstairs apartment mostly on the weekends. I live right under them and hear it all. She looked at Aunt G and smiled and said, "Other than that, they are a good couple." Then she whispered, "But you did not hear this from me." Happy to have helped with her investigative reporting, she strolled into the apartment building.

Aunt G could not wait to get back home to share her news. She shouted at my mother, "Charity you fool! That no-good man is married and has a baby on the way. Here you are laying up with him for free. What a fool you have been!"

Again, Mama refused to believe the worse. She shouted back, "I don't believe you. I love him, and he loves me."

Aunt G would not give up and reminded her. "But he treats you like dirt; hitting you, and the way he talks to you is a shame. He calls you crazy and stupid whenever he wants to."

Mama could not understand what Aunt G was talking about. "At least he loves me," she said. "He can't be married. He promised to marry me. He pays attention to me like I am special."

Aunt G shook her head. "You are just stupid!" she scorned.

Not long after Aunt G's investigation, my mother found out for herself that Big John was indeed married. He had recently married Gloria after promising to marry my mother. That must have been hard for my mother with me being on the way. His visits became less and less and eventually the visitations stopped. But when he did visit, they fought. He was rough with her, physically fighting her and accusing her of cheating on him. He just sat on the couch and said nothing to her. Finally, he disappeared without saying goodbye.

I finally was born, and my mother continued to search for answers for why things turned out the way they did with Big John. She could not find what she needed, so Charity (my mother) wandered the streets. She disappeared for days, sometimes weeks. Neighbors occasionally saw her walking the streets and talking to herself. Aunt G told me years later that after I was born, Aunt G took Big John to court for child support. Big John denied that I was his child in court and said that I was too light to be his child. Aunt G laughed and told him that skin tones changed as a child got older. DNA test proved that I was his child. The judge awarded Mama only twelve dollars a month for child support for me. Aunt G told him to take his money, stick it where the sun didn't shine and took us back home with her.

Aunt G always gave me preferential treatment. Sometimes, the other children in the house, got jealous. She did not call me as many names as she called them. However, she often told me that I look just like No-good Big John.

Aunt G did not tell Charity where Big John lived. But after he left, Charity searched for him. Sadly, for her, she could not find him even though he lived two blocks away. Charity searched for Big John day and night calling his name as she walked up and down the street in the neighborhood. She revisited the places they went together. She was brokenhearted and became depressed as a result of their break-up. When Charity was home she scared me, staring up at the ceiling like it had answers for her, mumbling to herself in a strange tone. "Wait till the battle is over; I will be free." She sang that tune over and over. She lost all interest in life and those around her, including us.

Chapter 7

Complex G

*I*t was obvious that Aunt G was such a complex woman. She kept a wall around her emotions. I felt like I was her daughter at times, until she would often remind me that I was on the street eating out of garbage cans when she found us. She would let me know that I was not special to her and not to think that I was. "You are only here because of my promise to my mother that I would take care of Charity's children," she said.

Aunt G had two biological daughters she did not raise, but I never heard anyone say who raised them. I did not understand why she took care of other people's children when she did not raise her own. People said that she was mean to her children as well. They spoke about how she talked badly to them and hit them, especially the darker daughter, Cheryl. She would hit Cheryl and say to her that she looked just like her no-good father. Aunt G hated Cheryl's father because he left her for another woman when she was sick with polio. Aunt G was unable to move for over a year.

But Aunt G said God provided a miracle when she was cured of her disease. She said that she made up in her mind after he left, never to trust a man ever again. She also said that nothing would ever get her down like that incident with her sickness and her husband. She said, "I told myself that I would be self-sufficient. I would work hard and get everything that I need."

Aunt G tried to teach Mama about men, but she did not listen. Aunt G said mama was too attractive for her own good and that was why she got in trouble with men. Mama was considered an attractive woman by anyone's standards; men followed her like bees to honey.

A year passed after Big John's disappearance, and Mama found another man. Aunt G was infuriated. "Who is this Spagnola that you have met and brought here to my house?" Aunt G was prejudice against anyone who did not look like her. Relatives said that the Mexican man Mama invited to the house was De-De's daddy, but De-De never met him. There was no information given to her about him at all. There was just the speculation that he may have been Mexican. Aunt G said that he was a Mexican (Spagnola as she called him).

My sister De-De was born two years after I was born. She was a beautiful fair skinned petite girl with soft, black long curly hair. She had those dark piercing eyes and big bright smile like Mama. She looked like she was a mixed breed which was how the relatives described her. Unfortunately, she was hated for her light complexion. Aunt G would constantly harass De-De, whenever she was around. Aunt G would yell at her, accusing her of stealing her money. "Get out of here with your yellow ass! I bet you stole my money. You are a big teef *(thief)*. I hate a teef *(thief)* I hate you and your Spagnola daddy, whoever he is. Do you know who your father is? No, you don't! Look at your yella *(yellow)* ass!"

The words coming from Aunt G made me cringe. It was true that no one had seen De-De father except Aunt G. But it just wasn't fair how or right that De-De was treated like she had done something wrong, just because she was born light-skinned. The harassment from Aunt G went on day and night; she was called yella and other names that were derogatory. Whenever she called De-De to her, she did not want her in her presence for an extended period. Aunt G would say what she had to say to De-De quickly. Afterwards she would say, "Get your yella ass away from me. Make me sick! You are going to be nothing because you came from nothing. Look at you. Who is your father? Oh, that's right! Nobody knows who he is!" She would let out a sinister-like laugh and continue with the verbal attack. "Now like I said, sit your yella ass behind down before I knock you down." Aunt G could not stand for De-De to be around her. She would become agitated just to look at her. No matter how Aunt G treated her, she laughed at her. She would laugh so loud and hard it made the rest of us laugh. When Aunt G spoke to her in the defaming way, I got pain in the pit of my stomach. Even though De-De laughed, we saw the hurt in her eyes and only laughed because she did the same.

Aunt G was cruel with information that she gave to us about our background or our mother. Often, she would say, "Charity, your mother, is trifling and sick in the head. She does not know who any of your fathers are, except you Vilma, and he is nothing to mention. She goes around in the street sleeping with men for free. She loves to have stray babies for me to take care of."

I would escape into one of my *foggy* moments wishing I could get away from everything and everyone. In my room, there was a small window three stories up. The window was in the back of the house, leading to a long dark stone wall that went to the ground. When I felt like disappearing, I looked out the window seeing the darkness all around me, making me dizzy. I thought to myself, *if I jumped into the hole I could disappear forever. Would anyone notice that I was gone?* I dismissed the thought after a few minutes and would leave the window. Hearing noise from my sisters always snapped me back to reality. It was five of us girls by then and we were wild as could be. We had lived with Aunt G for five years and often complained that she was tired of us, wanting us out of her house. "I am tired of these kid's. Queenie needs to come and get her grandchildren." By then, I had no emotion. I just wrapped myself in the *fog* in my head and forgot what I heard. We continued to play, oblivious to our reality and being unwanted.

Chapter 8

Gone

I woke up to the bright sun shining in my eyes burning them. There was a strange feeling in the house; it was quiet. I did not smell any breakfast and I wondered if I woke up too late to eat. *I had missed breakfast! Why did I sleep so late?*

Something did not feel right. There was an eerie feeling, quiet, no screaming or yelling going on. There was always noise, the sisters were always playing, jumping around, screaming and running through the house. What was going on? Where was everyone? I thought they got up early and was already outside playing. I told them not to go outside without me.

 I got out of bed, looked around the house and looked out of the window. I looked down onto the stoop and I still did not see them. I shouted out of the window for their names. I called Margaret's name first even though she was not the next oldest. De-De was older; however, Margaret was the most sensible one and De-De was always mischievous. I did not get an answer, so I yelled for Chie and Shy.

What were they doing? We always told them that they were not supposed to go off the stoop. They were all going to be in trouble if they left the stoop without permission. I continued to look out of the window, but I did not see any sign of them. I stretched out of the window as far as I could, looking up and down the street. Once again, I screamed their names as loud as I could.

I screamed for Aunt G, "Where is everybody Aunt G? I don't see them. I have been calling for them, but they did not answer."

"They are gone," she said.

"Gone?! Where?! I screamed.

"With their Gra Mother."

Gra Mother? I repeated in my mind. I felt panic rising in my chest, yet I tried to keep my cool. I *better not let her know that I am upset. Be still; don't cry,* I told my mind. I wanted to scream, but I didn't.

I heard Aunt G talking about Gra Mother coming to pick them up, but I thought she was just blowing off steam. I did not realize that she was really going to let her take them. I heard her telling some of our cousins, that Gra Mother needed to come and get these kids because they were her grandchildren.

Aunt G said that she was tired and taking care of all of us and it was too much for her.

Why did she let her take them and she could not stand Gra Mother? They argued all the time about Mama, her condition of being mentally ill and how she walked the streets. Aunt G tried to get Gra Mother to explain to her why she treated her own daughter with such disgrace. She said it was not her fault what happened, so why abandon her.

There were various stories concerning the two sisters Aunt G and Gra Mother. The story I remembered came from my cousins talking while sitting on Aunt G's couch. I heard their mother would treat Aunt G better than she did my Gra Mother. The story is that Aunt G's mind was stronger than her sisters. Her mother counted on Aunt G to help her around the house. Gra Mother's mind was on other things; she loved to go walking or out playing with the girls. She did not have a mind to help around the house. No matter how hard her mother tried to get her to help, she would complain that she did not want to help. She would run outside and not come back until all the work was done. They said she would be staring off into space like she was somewhere else.

The relatives called her lazy and a little touched in her mind. The two of them obviously did not love each other; heck they did not like each other. When they were around each other, all they did was argue about who was right and who was wrong. "Mother loved you more than me," Queenie would whine. "You were lazy!" Aunt G holler back. "You are still lazy and mean as a snake." It was not pleasant being around them. I also thought that they would start throwing blows at each other though I never saw them fist fight. Just a war of words that would cut anyone to the heart. Sadly, they didn't love, like sisters should. Both treated their children like they did not give birth to them. They did not raise their own children. My Mother was taken from my Gra Mother and given to her mother.

The family secrets had my head twisted. I was the truth detective, even though no one knew that I was searching out the truth. I could always trust that the same cousins would come by weekly, sit on the couch and tell all the secrets. They had Aunt G's Bacardi rum in a cup with Coca Cola and they talked. I had my same spot in the doorway and I listened.

Cousin Flossie, who lived around the corner, liked Aunt G. She was not afraid to talk back to her either. She would tell her when she was wrong about anything, drink Aunt G's liquor and go home afterwards. Julia was soft spoken except after a few drinks. She would start talking fast, telling all the secrets about the family. Then there was Nettie, always wore those short skirts. She would have a cigarette in one hand and a drink in the other hand. She smiled while they talked saying, "Tell me more" or "What? You don't say."

Chapter 9

Behind the Curtain

*T*he cousins visited with Aunt G on Saturday afternoon on this occasion. Aunt G went to her cabinet to get the liquor and then the soda. After she put ice in the cups for the ladies, one of the tenants called her to the phone and she walked out of the living room. She left the cousins alone with their drinks.

I heard Nettie say, "Let's have our drinks before she comes back and curses us out." Nevertheless, Aunt G returned quicker than they thought she would. She was fussing about the lazy tenants, took the bottle of rum, poured some Coca Cola in her cup, and took a big drink from her cup. Then she said, "I feel better now." She started talking about how hard it was for her to manage the building by herself and take care of Charity's children without any help. One of the cousins responded, "Aren't you getting money for those kids?"

That statement set Aunt G off. She barked back. "I don't need the government's money; I have my own money. I own this house and I have two other jobs. I gave the children a home when no one wanted them." She looked straight at them and asked, "What have you done for them besides run your mouths? I give the children money and take diligent care of them. The money I get for them is not enough to do everything that I do for them."

They did not try to argue back with her, because they knew that they could not win arguments with her especially after she had a few drinks in her. Aunt G sat down with them and continued to drink her rum and coke. The conversation started to go deeper as I listened behind the curtain. I was saying to myself, *please do not notice me.* Aunt G, Nettie and Flossie were drinking, telling secrets with each other, and my ears opened wide to hear all. As the ladies changed the tone of the conversation, I heard the most horrific story I had ever snooped to hear. As I stood behind the curtain listening, what I heard next had me shaking with fear and sweat. Their account of the story began like this and subject matter was my Gra Mother. Flossie said that she heard this story from her mother, Gra Mother's other sister Jonie. We just called her the Jehovah Witness. She never talked to anyone in the family except her own children.

Flossie began the horrific tale. "My mother told me that one hot dusty day, Queenie *(my Gra Mother)*, a free spirit loved walking down the old country roads in South Carolina where they lived. She was at the tender age of eighteen and did not like working on the inside of the house. She heard a voice speaking to her, "Hey Queenie, what's going on?" She was startled and almost jumped out of her skin, thinking she was alone. "What's wrong; what you jumping for? It's just me Cousin Bob."

"Oh, hey Bob; you scared me." Bob was her cousin, her mother's brother's son. He was 25 years old, did not work; just roamed around the neighbor looking for odd jobs to do to get money. He was described by family members as a tall, lanky funny looking fella. Bob was nice to all the little girls in the neighborhood, but the girls in the neighbor said it was a creepy nice.

He would make them feel uncomfortable by his creepy smile and always showed those yellow teeth. They did not like the way he would greet them by touching and squeezing them on their shoulders. He looked them straight in their eyes and it seemed like to the soul. My mother said his behavior would give a bad chill to your spine. He would not look away until we looked away. She went on to say he would also sneak up behind some of the girls, pinch them in their side and laugh a hideous laugh and walk away.

He said, "Hey gal. Where you are going? "Home Bob," Queenie responded. "Come on and take the short cut with me," Bob told her. Queenie did not give it a thought and she did not want to upset Bob. She had seen his mean streak. He beat up a man once who owed him a dollar. He beat the man so badly the man almost died. He beat him with his bare hands.

"The short cut would be nice; it's hot out here," responded Queenie. "I have been walking for a while and I am thirsty. I don't want Ma angry with me. She is waiting and looking for me Bob. I have been out too long." Well, Queenie and Bob took the shortcut through a long dusty road. The hot wind was blowing dust on her dress. She began to shake her dress to get the dust off. She could feel the dust hit her legs and feet as they walked. Bob was not saying anything which she found strange. He was always talking too much. There were old abandoned buildings on this road and Ma had warned her not to walk those roads alone. "It is not safe," she could hear her mother's voice in her head.

I am with Cousin Bob, she thought it should be okay.

"I sure am thirsty," Bob said. "Are you thirsty Queenie?"

"Yes, I am," she responded back to him.

"There is a well behind that old shed over yonder. Come on; let's get some water."

"That's okay Bob. I will be fine. I need to get back home before Ma gets angry with me. I have been out all day and I need to get my chores complete."

"Come on here Queenie. I will tell her you were with me; it will be fine."

Queenie felt a strange sensation in her stomach telling her that it was not okay to follow Bob, but against her better judgement she followed him anyway.

He explained that the well with the cool water was behind the building he pointed to. The old gray wood building looked like no one had lived there for a while. Queenie looked around and did not see any other people. It looked scary to her. She began to question where the well was, because she did not see it. Feeling uneasy, she walked a little further behind the building. Where did Cousin Bob go? He had disappeared and had stopped talking again. She began to search for Bob when all of a sudden, she felt hands grab her from behind. Someone had her by her neck. The hands were squeezing her neck tighter and tighter. What was going on?! Fear gripped her mind and body. The large hands had grabbed her and choked her neck until she could not breathe or scream. She twisted and turned trying to get away from the large hands. She even tried to kick away from the person but could not break free. The more she kicked and twisted to get away, the tighter the grip of the hand got.

The body that belonged to the hands began to press up against her so hard she could feel a bulge pressing in her back. He was crushing her small-framed one-hundred-pound body to the point that she was starting to feel pain in her back and neck. She was sweating from the heat outside and from fear inside her mind. Queenie could hardly breathe, and every breath was a struggle. Her mind was in a world wind. *Where was Cousin Bob? Why did he leave me here alone?* The smell from the sweat of the person choking her along with the heat was making her dizzy to where she felt like she was going to pass out.

Ma is going to kill me was all she could think about. *I need to get home! Help me somebody*! She screamed in her mind. *Mama help me! Cousin Bob help me*! As she continued to twist and turn, finally she was able to escape from the grip on her neck. She gasped hard and took a deep breath. She could finally see the face of the person who was attacking her. To her shock, oh no! It was Cousin Bob who had her in the choke hold! At this point she felt like her life was in danger. She had never seen her cousin this way. The expression on his face was that of a mad man. *Why was he trying to hurt me?* She thought. *Why was he pressing up against me like he was?* Fear had never gripped her mind and body like that before. But she knew that if she wanted to live, she had to fight to get out of that unpleasant situation. She mustered up a low scream, but no words would come out of her mouth.

She thrusted around like a wild cat, fighting with all of her might. Queenie felt like death was coming; she thought her cousin was about to kill her or in her mind something worse was about to happen. Queenie knew what was coming next would be her worst nightmare.

She could feel all of Cousin Bob's two hundred-pound body grab her tighter toward his. He suddenly grabbed her neck again with one big hand and choked her. He grabbed her neck tight enough that she almost fainted. She could see stars; her head was dizzy and hurting. Next, he pushed her to the ground hard and her head hit the dusty ground.

Dust flew into her eyes which mixed with her burning tears. Dust went into her mouth choking her more as she opened her mouth to scream. Dirt was everywhere all over her body. Still, Bob had his big dirty smelly hand around her neck. He moved the hand from her neck and covered her mouth to keep her from screaming. She was on the ground, head hurting, breathless, and unable to talk or scream. He pulled her dress up and raised Queenie's dress over her head, smothering her with the feeling of his hot, sweaty body on top of hers. His heavy breathing over her just made her even more hot and nauseated. The stench from his breath almost made her pass out. Her mind was going in circles, as she murmured, "Why Cousin Bob, why?" She began to go into a deep *fog*.

She did not know what to think or do. She was getting weak from struggling with Bob. He then ripped her dirty, once-white panties so hard from her little body, that the elastic ripped and burned the inside crease of her thighs. *He is going to crush me,* she thought. Gasping to catch her breath, struggling to get his body from top of her, she tried to keep his body from crushing her to death. *Oh God, I can't breathe he is too heavy,* she kept thinking. *My head is foggy. Where is my voice? I cannot talk! Why is Bob doing this? He has always been nice to me. What have I done to him to make him hurt me? Oh no Lord! Help me! What is that?* There was stinging, pressure and pain like she had never felt before. He had thrust his penis inside of her. It felt like she was being ripped apart from the inside out. She had never known a man in this way; Queenie was still a virgin.

He continued to thrust, his body moving fast and making a horrible sound; drool and sweat hit her face. After a while she allowed her mind to go somewhere else. She thought, *what will Mama say when I got home? She is looking for me I know.* The tortured rape seemed to last forever. Time had stopped. She thought that she would die right there under her cousin on that dusty ground. She believed that she passed out for a few minutes from the pain and the heat.

When Bob finally finished, he pulled out his penis, jumped up and looked down at Queenie. He saw that her dressed was pulled over her face so that he did not have to look at her. He pulled her dusty, dirty bloody dress from her face. He just kept looking at her lying there on that hard ground. Tears and dirt were mixed together all over her pain-stricken and terrified face.

Cousin Bob took her torn bloody panties and wiped her teared filled face with them. After he wiped her face, he tossed the panties to the side. Flossie took a breath and continued. Queenie said, "He pulled my dress down to smooth it out. Cousin Bob took those big dirty hands gave me a tender pat on my face. He smiled that Cousin Bob creepy smile that gave me a chill in my body that I will never forget. He bended down to my eye level and looked me right in my eyes. Spoke these words I will never forget. "Tell anybody gal and I'd kill ya." Then he got up smooth out his clothes like he was ironing them out walked away whistling a strange eerie tone.

I laid there on that cold ground, crying and hurting in my mind, body and soul. I felt like I was going to die. Once I stopped crying and my head was not dizzying anymore, I got off the ground and looked around to make sure that he was gone. I wondered if anyone saw me or was anyone looking for me. My head was aching, and my thighs throbbed like a toothache. The pain and burning sensation between my legs was almost unbearable. *How do I clean up all this blood running down my legs?* She looked at the blood on the ground as well. She was in so much pain bruised on her thighs and neck. I felt like I wanted to die."

Queenie (Gra Mother) was hurting in her body and in her heart. She thought again about what she could have done that made Cousin Bob hurt her the way that he did. She hated herself and her cousin. *Why did I walk with him behind that building?* She got up and tried to straighten out her clothes. She walked home, beaten battered, confused; constantly looking around as she walked making sure that Cousin Bob was not around. To her it was the longest walk of her life, even though it was only a half mile away from the house. Finally, she made it back home.

She made her way into the house without making a sound. Mama was at that old stove cooking as she always did. Mama did not look around to see her; she was too busy rushing around to finish cooking. She did not speak to her mother, yet she wanted her to notice her condition. In her mind, she was screaming, *look Mama; your baby is hurt! The one you never see? Look at your bloody torn baby, Mama! Oh God! I need you! Please help me Mama! Cousin Bob hurt me!* She cried on the inside and never muttered a word to her mother.

In shock that her mother did not notice her pain, she went into her room thinking, *she never notices me anyway. That's why I hate everybody around here. Does she notice that I will*

never be the same? Does she know that I am a dead person?
Queenie tore the blood and dust stained dress off. She said her
dress felt like it was burning her skin and she had to get it off.

She smelled the blood and dust. The memory of what
happened made her run to the toilet and throw up. She took a
basin of hot water and soap and scrubbed for an hour trying to
clean the blood and the pain away. After changing her clothes,
she took the dress outside and buried it in the ground like a
corpse. She went back into her room, crawled in the bed and
balled herself up into a knot fell into a deep sleep. Hours later,
her mother called her to go out into the garden and pick some
vegetables for supper. She said that she sucked it up and
suffered in silence.

Hearing Aunt G's voice snapped me back into my reality from
my shock and trance-like state of mind. Aunt G stated after the
rape, Queenie was never the same; she hated everyone. Aunt G
told the ladies the only other person she ever told what
happened to her was Aunt G. "She told me to never tell anyone,
but I could not hold the secret anymore. With taking care of
her daughter Charity and her children, this load is making me
weary." I was shocked and dared not move. If they saw me, I
knew I would be dead for sure. I felt paralyzed even though I
needed to move from that spot. *Is this real?* I felt like nothing
was real anymore. A great *fog* came over me. My legs were

numb, my head was foggy. I slowly moved away from the curtain and left the women to their conversations.

The question remained in my mind. *But why did Gra Mother hate Aunt G, especially if she told her about the tragic rape by her Cousin Bob?* I was always ease dropping on conversations of Aunt G's usual gossip in the living room. Aunt G's anecdote began like this. "Our mama who lived next door heard the screams of terror, ran into the house and saw the horror. In Gra Mother's arms was a child who was burned, bleeding and screaming! She snatched the baby from the arms of Gra Mother. From that day forward, Gra Mother was not allowed to be alone with my niece. Ma-Ma, Gra-Mother's six-month-old baby never seemed quite right in her head after the incident. How could a mother do such a thing? There was quiet in the room. When my mother became ill, my sister got Charity back and continued to beat her child every day. My mother on her dying bed made me promise to take care of Charity."

After hearing this one, I needed more information. The stories were never pleasant for me to hear, but I needed to hear them. I needed to know why my family behaved the way that they did. I overheard the same story but, in more details, and it made me dizzy to the point of almost passing out. My cousins were talking about how Gra Mother abused my mother Charity when she was a baby at six months old. They were talking about the hate my Gra Mother had for her. My Great Gra

Mother was visiting her daughter, my Gra Mother, and my mother. They said, "The baby cried all the time and this day, she could not get Charity to stop crying."

My Gra Mother was changing Charity's diaper. My Gra Mother got angry with her and grabbed her up in a haste of anger by her little arms. Then she took her naked bottom to the hot stove and placed her on it! The baby screamed in terror and pain. My Great Gra Mother was about to knock on the door when she heard screaming from my mother. So, she ran into the house! To Great Gra Mother's shock and surprise, My Gra Mother had placed my mother's naked bottom on the hot stove. When great Gra Mother asked her why, she screamed, "The little bitch would not stop crying!"

Great Gra mother snatched my screaming mother from my Gra mother, her daughter. She had burn marks all over her bottom and was taken to get medical care. From that day on, My Gra Mother was not allowed to go around my mother. One of the cousins said, "Now she has Charity's children. Is anyone going to rescue them from *that* monster?"

Chapter 10

Gra Mother's House

My sisters had been living with Gra Mother for six months. It seemed like forever to me since I had seen them. Something bad happened to Shy while there. When Shy was five years old, she was playing with her favorite ball on the sidewalk and it rolled away from her. She ran, focused on getting her ball back and did not see the oncoming car. The lady that was driving the car tried to stop to keep from hitting Shy, but she was driving too fast to stop on time.

The speeding car hit my sister hard, tossed her in the air and she was thrown over a wired fence. Her small body hit the concrete and she laid on the ground motionless. She was rushed to the nearby hospital. Shy had a punctured lung, both legs were broken from her hips and she was placed on the critical list at the hospital.

Mama went to the hospital every day to feed Shy ice cream to get her to eat. She laughed with Shy and told jokes to cheer her up. The doctors put a body cast on Shy which started at her chest and went down to her toes. I heard that Gra Mother got money from the lady's insurance company for Shy but did not do anything for Shy with the money. She spent Shy's money on her other daughter and grandchildren. I heard horrible stories about my Gra Mother; therefore, I was afraid to meet her.

"Come on; let's go!" demanded Aunt G. "Where are we going?" I stammered, even though I knew we were off to Gra Mother's. I just did not want to leave. The thought of looking at her gave me chills, made me sick and dizzy. I thought I was better off not knowing her. I felt uneasy about the girls living with her.

We got on the bus to Gra Mother's house and when we arrived, Aunt G knocked on the door. To my horror, an old, short black-as-the night woman, answered the door. Her face looked so odd to me. It had black spots and black spots had white spots on top of them. She also had deep, long wrinkles. Although she was a petite woman, in my mind, she was a tall, ugly witch.

As Gra Mother opened the door, I felt a cold breeze hit my body and fear hit my heart. I looked up, hoping that she did not notice me. She sure did look mean. Gra Mother did not crack a smile or speak. She opened the door and walked away from us. She turned back to my Aunt G and muttered, "What do you want G?" Aunt G said, "I brought her by to visit her sisters. I will be back to get her later." Gra Mother did not even look at me. I was scared because I had never seen anyone look like that before. It was dark and ashy skin that looked like she had not put any lotion on her face in a long time. She looked like one of those witches I had seen on television, except she was a black witch. I stopped looking at her before she got mad at me.

People said she could put roots on you by looking at you. I heard she went to the Root lady often for answers and spells to put on people. She had a strange smell like the Root house. It resembled a strong perfume that would choke you. When she returned from the Root house, she carried strange toys and lotions, chanting, "I will fix them." I hoped she had not fixed my sisters.

I looked around for my sisters but only saw a kitchen set in the middle of the floor and four chairs. One of the chairs had a big steel chain with a lock on it. The refrigerator had a big rope chain with locks around it as well. I turned around and there was Shy, my youngest sister who was five years old at the time. Shy was in a small, cold dark bedroom by herself. She was unable to move due to her body cast from the accident. I saw the results of that awful accident as my sister laid in the top bunk bed. She was frail and the sad look on her face held dried tears. She was wearing a dirty body cast from her waist down, her toes sticking out from the cast. She was shivering from being cold and being in pain. I looked at her and turned away. I did not want her to see the look of horror on my face. When I got up my nerve, I went back to Shy's room. I tapped the cast to feel it and it made a thump, hollow sound. The cast was hard to the touch. I was wondered if she could feel pain when I tapped it. It was difficult for me to look down at Shy in that bed.

"Hi, Shy." She looked up at me with pitiful pleading eyes. She was under weight, like she had not eaten in days. I felt a lump in my throat, pain in my chest. She opened her mouth to speak, a whisper came out, and said, "Help us." She was too afraid to say anything else. I left the room to find my other sisters.

They told me that Shy cried and moaned all the time because of the pain. Gra Mother refused to give her pain medicine. Margaret said when she wet herself, Gra Mother got upset and beat her toes with an extension cord. Shy being unable to move, endured the beating and screams. Unable to take herself to the bathroom, she was given a bed pan, but she still needed assistance with the bedpan. When Shy wet herself, sometimes she was made to lay in it, until one of my sisters cleansed her. Gra Mother did not care, in fact said, "Let her lay in it for a while, that will teach her."

I spotted a hole in the back of her cast by her bottom. I guessed it was for her to use her bowels and be cleaned. Although, I doubt the cleaning part happened as often as needed. I did not know what to do. I was only ten years old. All I could do was stare at Shy and my sisters. The *fog* in my head was taking over. I was motionless and powerless. The screaming Gra

Mother directed my attention. "Shut up! I am about to give you something to scream about!" I acted like I did not hear her. I turned my back hoping that she was not referring to me. I got up the nerve to look around and go into the other room without her noticing me. Gra Mother was placing Shy, cast and all, in a cold tub of water with ice cubes in it.

Shy was screaming, squirming and hitting at Gra Mother. She was terrified of the iced water bath. It looked like My Gra Mother was trying to drown Shy. She slammed Shy's little body in the tub of freezing water. She pulled the extension cord off the television and hit Shy's naked, wet frail upper body. Shy squalled so loud it sent chills through my body. Petrified I peed in my pants. When she was finished torturing Shy, she hollered for eight-year-old Margaret. "Come on, you are next. I need to get that funny motion off you. Filthy dirty girls, I can't clean trash. You are all dirty trash. If I can't clean the trash off you, I can beat it out of you all." She reached for Margaret, but Margaret was strong and pulled away from her grip. Giving her the fight of her life, Gra Mother was not able to hold Margaret all the way in the cold water. As hard as Margaret fought, she lost the battle. Eventually, Gra Mother threw her in the cold tub and beat her with the extension cord. She cried loud and hard. I saw the whelps on her body from the leather extension cord.

"Since you all gave me a tough time," Gra Mother warned, "I am going to beat you until you learn." She reached for six-year-old Chie next. "Look what happens when you are filthy dirty girls. Come here." Chie sat in the chair at the kitchen table, following her orders. Gra Mother tied her to the chair and Chie did not fight back. "I am going to show you all what happens when you disobey an order from me. I am going to punish her for Margaret giving me a hard time. You will do what I tell you to do." Chie had a look of terror on her face. I turned away again; I could not look at her. Once Chie was placed in the dining room chair, my Gra Mother took a steel chain with a lock and locked her to the chair. Gra Mother then got the extension cord and beat her. She screamed for what seemed like forever. Eventually the sounds stopped coming out of her mouth. I looked at her and she looked like she was sleep. Unfortunately, she wasn't, but unconscious from the brutal beating.

Gra mother walked away, without saying a word. She left Chie slumped over in the chair, arms bleeding and swollen. Gra Mother came back into the kitchen, to release Chie from the chained chair. As Gra Mother unlocked the chains, Chie woke up. Gra Mother said in a calm but eerie voice, "I am doing yawl a favor, by cleansing you with water and beating the filth and funny motion out of you. I can smell it on you. Come here, Margaret. Get in the tub again; you are not clean enough."

Margaret surrendered, as she was beaten and being scrubbed with a rag. Gra Mother acted like she did not get any satisfaction in her beating of my sister. Margaret struggled to catch her breath while trying to stay out of the water. She gave up the fight and let Gra Mother beat her until she got the satisfaction she was looking for. Gra Mother finally got tired and let Margaret go.

I looked over at my Gra Mother, after she finished beating my sisters, waiting for her to snatch me up. She never looked my way. It was as if I was invisible to her. Her evil mission of beating and tormenting my sisters was over. Gra mother stopped the punishment and took a break. She proceeded to cook. *Thank God, she stopped*, I thought. I switched my mind from the beatings and thought about what she was cooking. I was hungry.

Gra mother cooked baked sweet potatoes. She placed three sweet potatoes stacked on one plate. I reached for a sweet potato, being careful because I expected it to be hot. To my surprise it was cold, and half cooked. I did not say anything, just bit into it. I could not even chew it. "Eat!" she screamed. Everyone picked up the raw sweet potato and ate. I was unable to speak. I felt like I was watching a horror movie, while eating my raw sweet potato. That night we all went to bed wounded.

Aunt G came back to get me three days later. As I was leaving with Aunt G, my sisters peeped at me behind the door. I could not imagine what was about to happen to them as I was about to leave. I read the language of their eyes. They did not speak, but I heard them loud and clear, *please do not leave us! Help us!* On the way back to Aunt G's house, I told her that Gra Mother was beating my sisters. Aunt G did not say anything. She gave me a look with no expression, yet I knew that what I told her was no surprise.

I felt guilty watching my sisters be abused while I was not. Gra Mother did not look or acknowledge me at all. I was protected because I lived with Aunt G. Margaret told me that the beatings and harsh words continued day and night. She punished them with cold-water baths for cleansing of the "funny motion." The looks of horror and pain on my sister's faces were etched in my mind day and night.

I dreamed about my sisters, especially Shy's frail body. She looked like a hurt doll lying in a dirty bunk bed. Why was she in the top bunk bed? Gosh, her sheets were dirty. I did not know what was real anymore living in this *fog*. I reached out to touch Shy in my dreams. I tried to touch her, but I drew my hand back quickly. I can't touch Shy; she is dirty. I hate dirt and I hate feeling dirty. I can smell Shy's blood in my dream. I felt helpless and lost. What could *I* do about it? I needed to help them.

I awoke from my dream, thinking how she could beat Shy with the cast on. Shy was beaten about her arms and her toes. I saw all the scars from the extension cord. I thought about how she wet her bed and I got sick to my stomach, running to the bathroom to throw up. I forced the thoughts to leave my mind and tried to concentrate on something else.

I did not stop asking Aunt G day and night to help my sisters. I told her everything I saw, the cruelty, all the beatings. It was time for school to start again and Chie was six years old in school. While she was in class, a teacher noticed that her arm had an odd shape. It was also swollen, black and blue. The teacher asked Chie to come closer to her. When she went to touch Chie's arm she screamed in pain. She took Chie to the nurse's office and the nurse said, "I believe her arm is broken." Her arm was twice the size it should have been and was black and blue in color. The nurse asked Chie what happened. Chie crying and shaking explained, "My Gra Mother tied me to the kitchen chair with a chain and beat me with the extension cord from the television." The teacher was horrified and called the police. They called my Gra Mother to the school and asked her what happened to the child. She said, "She must have fallen." Gra Mother left the school and went home.

Chie was taken to the hospital; her arm was broken in three places with compound fractures. The hospital called the Department of Child Protective Services. Chie was placed in an orphanage. They went to Gra Mother's house and took Margaret along with Shy. No charges were brought against Gra Mother. When Child Protective Services picked up the girls, Gra Mother laughed and said, "Get these filthy children out of here."

Margaret, Shy and Chie were placed in the State Institution for Orphans but were separated from each other. De-De was on her way to visit our sisters. She had run away a long time ago. When De-De saw the State car arrive at the house for my sisters, she left crying. De-De ran away to her Godmother's house, Ms. Watkins, who was a very nice lady in her late fifties. De-De often ran to Ms. Watkins to escape the beatings. Whenever Gra Mother reached for De-De, she ran and stayed away. Ms. Watkins took De-De in, fed her and gave her nice clean clothes to wear. She treated De-De as if she was her daughter.

My sisters were gone, but safe from the beatings of Gra Mother. I asked Aunt G when she was going to get them from the state home. She just looked at me and walked away. But I asked every day for two years.

Chapter 11

The Promise

I was in Aunt G's bedroom, which was next to the living room. I hid behind the long, thick gray curtains. My heart was beating fast as I listened with hope to her conversation. "I must go and get Charity's children from the orphanage home," I heard. Aunt G left and was gone the entire day. I was afraid of being left alone. I thought I would die if I had to go to Gra Mother's house.

Just as I was about to panic, the door opened. My sisters walked through the door, laughing, and talking. What a surprise! Aunt G went and got my sisters from the orphanage. They looked happy and healthy. Margaret was ten years old, Chie was eight and Shy was seven. Shy was still small, but she had shed her cast and was walking. I was screaming on the inside. I was so happy that tears rolled down my checks. I tried to speak, but nothing came out of my mouth for a few seconds. After I got over the shock, I grabbed and hugged each of them. We ran and played as if we were there together all the time.

We were all together; no more beatings. Aunt G gathered us together right away to make an announcement. "I promised my mother on her deathbed that I would take care of Charity, and any children she had. Understand that if it were not for the promise, I made to my mother, I would have left you all in the home with my crazy sister Queenie. Do not give me any trouble, or you will go back with her or back to the orphanage." We all just walked away from Aunt G without a word.

She continued to mumble to herself. "I took Charity from Queenie. I raised her the best way that I could. She had five girls with different fathers and no husband. She is now a woman, crazy in her mind walking the streets. God help her. God help us. I do not know what to do."

Aunt G often threatened us with words from the promise to her mother on her mother's deathbed. The promise helped me to understand why we were with Aunt G. She turned to me and said, "Your mother is crazy and none of you except you, Vilma has a father. Well, you don't have much of a father," she reminded me. "Your father, Vilma does not want you. He left you at the courthouse. You all will amount to nothing. You came from nothing. You have no choice but to be nothing."

The expressions of hate and resentment on Aunt G's face towards us when she was spitting her poison always left me feeling worthless. She was unhappy with the outcome of her own life. She often spoke regret concerning her unhappy marriage, how she hated men, how one of her daughter's

Cheryl was an alcoholic and the disappointment of her. She had two biological children of her own; one she loved and one she was always upset with.

"Time for me to tell you what you need to do," she explained to me one day as we sat in the kitchen. "I must work. You are the oldest," she spoke while pointing her wrinkled finger in my face, almost touching the tip of my nose. "It is your responsibility to take care of them."

I accepted the task, without a thought of how. I listened as she went on. "Make sure you get them up for school, at five am each morning. Eat breakfast by six am, clean the house, cook, and make sure homework is done. It better be done when I get home from work. If not, you are all going back to the home." The home is what we always called the orphanage.

Aunt G worked all the time, so I was in charge. By this time of year, it was hot and humid outside. We opened all the windows in the large apartment. School was going to be out in two days. We lived on the fourth floor of the brownstone building. I opened the front windows and put speakers from the record player in the window. I blasted Michael Jackson's "Rocking Robin" record. Our friends could hear the music playing on the street. Crowds would form in front of our stoop, while the children danced in front of the house. I was bouncing to the rhythm of the music, shouting, singing to the people below along with Michael Jackson. "Go rocking robin go! Rocking robin! Rock, rock, rock!" Wow what fun; singing, having a wonderful time and freedom! I was consumed with the smell of summer and the breeze blowing. I felt free as the song rung out loud. I look down from my window and saw the people dancing and enjoying the music.

Someone looked up at me and shouted, "Miss G is coming! Hey Vilma! Miss G is coming!" Oh God! My heart stopped, and I snatched the speakers out of the window. In a frantic effort to clean up, I straighten up the apartment as much as I could and as fast as I could. Aunt G came in frowning as usual. She looked tired and worn out. I greeted her at the door with a smile and a "Hello Aunt G."

"What have you riff-raffs been doing? Why is there no dinner on the stove? The house is a mess. Could you not have cleaned the house at least and have something on the stove for me to eat? I worked all day, sixteen hours. No one thought enough of me to even make a sandwich or anything for me? Did you feed the girls?"

"Yes, Aunt G."

"You could not leave me one crumb? I let you all stay in my house for free. I worked all day and come home tired. At least you could have ironed my work clothes. You are good for nothing with your Big John looking self! You look like your no-good father! Get out of my face!" she screamed.

I made sure everyone went to bed early after washing up. Then, I washed and ironed Aunt G's work clothes for the next day. I peeped into Aunt G's room to check in on her. I saw her sitting on her bed with her head hung down. She did not look big that night; just sad and worn out. I wanted to reach out to her, but I didn't. She might have cursed me out. I left her to herself and went in my room.

I felt sorry for her having to deal with us. Aunt G was a faithful employee. Each morning she got up at five am to go to work. Looking at how worn out she was that night, I was glad her day off was the very next day. That night I went to bed thinking about Mama as well. I missed our mother and wondered what she was doing. We had not seen her in months. I fell asleep and woke up in the middle of the night, hearing Aunt G yelling at Mama. At first, I thought I was dreaming. But it was not a dream, just a living nightmare.

Chapter 12

Mama Please

*A*unt G yelled at Mama. "It's crazy! You walk the streets all the time like you are a mad woman. Walking up and down the dang gone street, screaming like you have lost your mind." The neighbors told Aunt G that Mama slept in cars of strangers. As Aunt G yelled, I looked up at Mama to see her reaction. She was chanting, standing in the door way of our bedroom looking at the ceiling. I wondered, *was she in pain and what she chanting about*? I believed Mama was always in pain and that was her way of dealing with it.

I stood so close to her I could almost touch her. But she did not see me standing there. She was in a trance, chanting out loud in a painful tone. "Oh, Lord, look in my mouth. Oh Lord, look in my mouth."

I just stared at her scared, wondering, what was wrong with her? When I went to bed, her words rang in my head... *"Oh, Lord look in my mouth."* I closed my eyes and strange things filled my mind. I saw a man, with a dog in my room standing beside my bed. He had the big dog on a leash. He did not speak just stood there in my room looking at me like they were protecting me. I felt safe and at peace with that vision in my head. I looked at the man and dog and heard whisperings in my mind, repeatedly. *Wait until the battle is over. Wait until the battle is over.* Was God telling me that when this was over, I was going to be okay? I hoped I was not going crazy like Mama. Eventually, I drifted off to sleep again with my sisters next to me.

The next morning, I was awakened out of my sleep at 6:00am. Aunt G was yelling at us. "You lazy riff-raffs; get up and eat! If you don't get up in five minutes, you are not going to get anything to eat." That morning she was in one of her bad moods. "I am so sick and tired of yawl. Now get your lazy behinds up." I ignored Aunt G's words and concentrate on the food she had prepared for us. There was crispy fried fatback meat, grits with the fatback grease poured over it and tomato sardines. No one cooked like Aunt G! I was hungry, so I rushed to prepare plates for my sisters.

While eating, Cheryl, Aunt G's youngest daughter walked in smiling. She was always smiling even though she had lots of reasons not to. She was another member of our family going through changes in her life. Cheryl lived in the first-floor apartment. "How are you doing Gail?" she greeted her mother, in a friendly tone.

Aunt G looked up at Cheryl, like she was the lowest thing she had ever seen. Cheryl was twenty-eight years old and a tall skinny dark beauty. I liked her short hair which she curled with a curling iron. If you saw Cheryl, you saw her security blanket, which was her can of Miller beer. From the looks of her, we could tell she had been out drinking all night long.

Aunt G was disappointed in her youngest daughter and never failed to tell her. She would start with a disapproving look. Still Cheryl smiled at her and sat down to eat. Then Aunt G started to complain to her. "You riff raffs been out all-night long. Why don't you get a job? Why don't you stop sleeping with Jimmy, my super for my building? Look at you! You are a no-good mess. You will never amount to anything. I am so sick and tired of you. Keep it up and I am going to put your black butt out of my house. Why did you leave your children by themselves while you went out partying?"

Aunt G kept coming with more questions and complaints. "Did you see your youngest child? Do you know that he is going through problems? He cries all the time and cannot sleep. The doctor said that he is hooked on alcohol, because you drank while you were pregnant. Take your dirty sick children with you!" She screamed.

Cheryl smiled halfway at Aunt G. but the expression on her face changed to embarrassment. I saw how the hurtful words had penetrated her heart. She tried to undo the smile before Aunt G's next attack of words. "Where have you been? You are no - good just like your no-good father. That's why I left him. He stayed out all night with other women. You are nothing and will never be anything. You hear me Cheryl?"

Cheryl got up from the table and walked out without saying anything to Aunt G. Then Aunt G looked at me. "What are you looking at? You always snooping around like the FBI. Get out of my face!"

I went outside to get away from her, even though it was hot out. I looked for my sisters. I told them not to go off the stoop, but they were hard headed for sure. I walked up the street and saw some friends and asked if they had seen them.

"What yawl doing; just hanging? Have you seen my sisters?"

Their response was, "Yeah, they around the block."

When I walked around the corner, I saw a crowd of people gathered around two girls arguing. I looked closer and it was Margaret. She did not take any mess. I told Margaret to come on home with me. I did not like fussing because it made me nervous. Margaret listened, and we headed home. The crowd and a large black tall girl about six feet followed her. My heart raced as the crowd cursed and threw threats at Margaret. "I am going to kick your butt this day Margaret! You think you so cute!"

We did not stop walking until we arrived in front of our house. The big girl shoved Margaret and a fight broke out. Margaret did not hesitate and hit the girl. Then she held her down on the ground and gave her a real good beating. Margaret's punches landed on the girl's face, one after the other. When they got up off the ground, I tried to stop the fight by getting in between them. All a sudden, I felt a fist hit my eye. Ouch; that hurt! I got out of their way since Margaret was throwing punches like a mad boxer. She connected her fist to the big girl's face again and again. This time, the girl fell to the ground and gave up. "You win fair and square!" She cried out and ran off.

Our other sisters heard what was going on and they headed home from where they were. When we went inside, they all laughed and pointed at my face. "What happened to you Vilma?" De-De laughed.

"I was trying to break up the fight between Margaret and that big giant of a girl." I explained the whole ordeal to them. They just continued to laugh.

"Margaret punched you in your eye good, Vilma," De-De said. I looked in the mirror at my big black eye and had to laugh at myself. We laughed so hard that Aunt G came in the room.

"What are you riff-raffs doing now?" She took one look at me. "Lord what happened to you, Vilma?"

"Goody-Two shoes got in the middle of Margaret's fight," Dede said, "and got punched in her eye, by Margaret."

Laughing Aunt G said, "I bet you will stay out of the way next time, won't you?" Throwing me an ice pack from the refrigerator, she said, "Here put this ice on your stupid face. Ha-ha-ha! Charity's riff-raffs. I don't know what I am going to do with yawl. I just don't know." Aunt G walked away laughing.

We ate our lunch and my sisters went back outside to play. I stayed on the stoop to keep watch on them. It got late and was time for dinner. Yum; I smelled the food that Aunt G was cooking! There were pork neck bones, white rice, gravy with onions, and collard Greens. I fixed my plate first to make sure that I got all the gravy I wanted on my rice. Afterwards, I fixed plates for my sisters. Then, we sat down to eat at the table.

They finished eating and ran off to play, even though I told them to help wash dishes. I washed the dishes, made sure that the kitchen was clean. Aunt G came into the kitchen looked at the clean pots. "You riff-raffs ate all the food? Where is my plate? Did you think that I did not want to eat after I cooked the food?"

Honestly, I did not think to leave Aunt G any food. When I saw food, it reminded me of the lack of food in the past. My sisters and I had the feeling that we must eat it all, to not be hungry later. Aunt G screamed that we did not leave her a crumb, calling us selfless good for nothings. "Damn! What did I get myself into?" She asked herself.

I felt bad for not leaving her food and could not explain why. Aunt G never taught me how to wash her dishes. And we could never do anything right for her. "Look at this mess! You can't even wash dishes right. Get out of my face!" I left Aunt G's presence feeling like I was not worth much and was good for nothing. I bet next time, I would make sure we left her some food. I would wash the dishes right and clean the kitchen. I wanted to show her that I was perfect and one day, she would be happy with me. I left to go outside, because I had to get away from her and that foul mood. With my great plans in my mind, I went on the corner to hang out with some friends.

Chapter 13
Mercy Pool

We loved going to Mercy Pool in the summer time. Aunt G would give us money to pay at the pool and it only costed fifty cents to swim all day. Everyone in Brooklyn went to the same pool on scorching summer days. I would find our swim suits, gather the girls, dress them and head to the pool. It was a terrific opportunity to get away from Aunt G screaming all day.

Once Aunt G had given each of us our pool money, I would get it and keep it. Everyone was excited except Shy. She never got excited about anything and was always quiet. But when she was with me, she was content.

We began our hour long walk to the city pool on that hot sunny day. As the sun beamed down on our heads, we were sweating and hot. My sisters started complaining. "We hungry Vilma."

Well, I decided to take our pool money, which was a total of $2.50, and stop by a corner store for food. I bought two hero sandwiches, chips, and a grape and orange soda for us. We ate as we walked, laughing, talking, and having a great time. As Shy ate her portion, she held onto me for dear life. She did not talk much, after being hit by a car when she was five. She also got tired fast, so I picked her up and put her on my back. We continued our walk to the pool area.

A few yards from the pool area, we could hear the laughter of the other children. We got to the pool entrance and I remembered we had spent all our money on food. "We are about to play a game," I told them, "called climb the fence." I told the girls that we must climb the tall wire fence to get in. Immediately, they looked afraid, so I said, "Don't be afraid. It's okay. I will climb first, then De-De will help you up. I will catch you once you are over." They agreed to do it because they had so much trust that I would not do anything to hurt them.

I climbed the fence first, excited in anticipation of the fun we were to have. De-De helped Margaret over the fence, but she eagerly jumped over by herself. She was a tom boy and it was no problem for her. But Chie needed help with her short legs. She started to climb while De-De pushed her from her bottom. I caught Chie as she jumped over the fence and almost fell backwards trying to catch her. When I stumbled, we all laughed at how silly I looked.

It was now Shy's turn to climb. She looked at me with fright in her eyes, but I reassured her that it okay. "Shy, De-De will help you climb all the way up." Shy nodded and began to climb. De-De was right behind her to push her up from her bottom with her hands and to make sure she did not fall. I climbed halfway back up the fence from the other side to guide her as well. Mission accomplished! We all made it over the fence without a hitch and paying the fifty-cent fee. It was time for fun!

De-De and Margaret were about to take off, but I stopped them and gave them instructions. "Be careful. Meet me in two hours at the front gate. And do not go in the deep end of the water." As they took off running, I screamed, "Do you hear me?"

They just kept running with no response. They knew how to swim; Chie and Shy stayed by my side. They could not swim and were too young to be left alone. They were just seven and eight years old. We sat on the edge of the baby pool area where I put their feet in the water to cool them off. I held on to my secret, that at twelve years old, I had not learned to swim yet.

Looking over the pool area, it was crowded with inner city kids. I was hardly able to see the water; so many black faces jumping around. Everyone was splashing, laughing and having fun. You had the freedom to laugh and thrash around; throwing each other in the water. The pool was outside in the opening, and the sun shone down right in the middle of the pool. There was supposed to be a life guard, but I had never seen one at the pool. If something bad occurred, who would help us? We took risks to have fun. A life guard in the inner-city pools was unheard of. No one cared if black children knew how to swim or even drown for that matter.

I wanted to put my feet in the cool water after the long hot walk too. De-De and Margaret were off playing with their friends. Shy and Chie were sitting on the side of the pool with their feet in the water. They did not make a move without me. Before I could think another thought, two boys came running toward me laughing and grabbed at me. I jumped up as fast as I could and screamed, "Stop!" I knew what they were up to; they liked throwing the girls in the pool. I ran from them because I could not swim.

"Come on girl; get in the water."

"No, leave me alone. I will get in when I am ready. Please stop!" I demanded. "I am not playing with you!"

I ran while screaming, "Stop!" I was afraid of being thrown in the water. I ran feet first into a wall. "Ouch! Dang it!" I hit my toes on the big stone wall. Oh, it hurt badly like a toothache. My toes felt broke, but I did not look at them right then. When I screamed out in agony, the boys ran off laughing. I disregarded the pain and got back with my sisters, Chie and Shy.

I stood Chie up in the kiddie pool; she liked it. She was smiling and splashing as I held her up in the shallow part of the water, which did not go past her waist. I tried the same thing with Shy, but she screamed for dear life. She begged and cried, "Please stop! Water hurt!" I did not stop to think that she was afraid of the water due to what happened to her in the past. I had forgotten about when Gra Mother put her in cold water and then beat her. I pleaded to her, "It's okay Shy. I will not let anything happen to you. It's just water. See?" "It's cold! Please stop!" She cried again, so I stopped trying to convince her. She looked at me with such fright in her eyes. Giving up, I sat her back on the side of the pool.

Suddenly, we heard someone shout, "Doo-doo!" The children in the pool screamed, splashed around and swam out of the pool. They were laughing and jumping out of the pool because one of the children in the pool had pooped in the pool! The poop floated to the top causing a big commotion. It made everyone run and jump out of the pool like they saw a snake. What a funny sight to see and hear! My sisters and I laughed until tears came out of our eyes and our stomachs hurt. It was two o'clock and time to start home.

I dried off Chie and Shy with a towel. Margaret and De-De showed up as they should for once and we headed back home. We were tired and hungry and did not have any money because we spent it on the way walking to the pool. "Come on let's hurry, so we can eat at home," I said. Shy was too tired to walk, and she reached her little arms for me to pick her up. I picked her up and placed her on my back. Shy was not heavy since she was not the normal size for a seven-year-old.

We walked for an hour and when we arrived at the house, the first voice we heard was Aunt G's. "Come on and eat riff-raffs." We climbed up the three flights of stairs and my mind was on the tasty food I smelled. Aunt G fussed a lot, but she made sure we always had food to eat and plenty of it. This time she cooked ham hocks, collard greens and rice. "Fix my plate; I'm hungry!" Margaret screamed. I told them to go wash their hands, while I fixed the plates.

My sisters got back in the kitchen and we sat down to eat. That food was good, and the ham hock was big and meaty. I ate my big ham hock halfway down to the bone, with my rice and gravy. I devoured my collards last. I was hungry, so I ate my food fast. We all ate our food sort of fast, like someone was going to take our food away from us. While the girls finished their meals, I washed the dishes. It was quiet in that kitchen and I did not hear a peep from the table while they ate.

When they were finished, they jumped up from the table and ran to the door. All I heard was little feet running down the stairs as they went back outside to play. "Don't go off the block!" I yelled. To my surprise, Shy went outside too. After I finished cleaning the kitchen, I went outside to check on my sisters. It must have been one hundred degrees outside. Shy was sitting on the stoop by herself, with her favorite winter coat on. "Shy," I asked," why do you have on your coat? It's hot out here. Take off your coat." She did not answer; just squeezed the coat tighter.

Everyone made fun of Shy; called her strange because she did not like being around people, except for me. She stuck to me like glue. She was quiet and intimidated by people. My sisters made fun of Shy also. "Is she crazy, wearing that old wool coat all the time?" They asked me. "Does she know that it's summer?"

No one understood that the coat was a source of a security for Shy. She wrapped the coat tightly around her body for protection from the world. No one tried to take the coat from Shy because we did understand that it made her happy, if there was happiness for her, the coat seemed to do it. I just left her alone; I got hotter looking at her. But I did sit next to her to keep her company. It would be getting dark soon, so I called my sisters to come back inside.

Chapter 14
Summer

We loved the summer because we could go out every day playing, laughing, and having a fun time. We got up when Aunt G called us for breakfast each morning at 6:00am. She always made the perfect breakfast; good, hot food no matter the weather. After breakfast in the summer, she told us to go outside; get out of the house and stay out all day.

"Do not run back and forth in and out of these doors," she bellowed. "If you are outside, stay outside. Stop swinging my doors back and forth!"

Did she think we could break those steel doors? She gets on my nerves! I never answered her back out loud; just in my head. I went outside just to get away from her mouth. *What did she expect us to do outside all day?* We were to go out in the morning and not return until right before twilight. We received two meals a day, breakfast and dinner. We had to fend lunch for ourselves, butt Aunt G gave us two dollars. We bought a hero sandwich, grape soda and chips from the corner store and still had one dollar and forty cents left for the day. *But why does she fuss all the time about everything and everybody? Is she ever happy or satisfied about anything?*

Well, on one of her good days, Aunt G said that she was taking us on summer vacation at her job to the Waldorf Astoria, a luxury hotel in Manhattan, New York. It was the original hotel on Fifth Avenue near 34th Street. The Waldorf Astoria is still known for lavish dinner parties and galas. It is often at the center of political business conferences and fundraising schemes involving the rich and famous. Celebrity Frank Sinatra kept a suite at the Waldorf Astoria, which tells you how extravagant and exclusive it was. The hotel was beautiful, and Aunt G would brag about where she worked all the time. "I don't have time for riff-raff. I work at a place with the rich and famous," she would brag.

"I am going to take you riff-raff out and show you how the real-world lives." Aunt G often brought home all sorts of goodies from her work; towels, sheets, and food. I often wondered how she carried all that stuff on the train. When it was time for us to leave for our vacation, I packed our bags, one small bag for each of us. I made sure we had our swim suits. We were ready, all five of us; I was twelve years old, Margaret ten, De-De nine, Chie eight and Shy seven. We were excited to go to the big hotel and be big shots too.

We walked two blocks to catch the C train on the way to Manhattan as Aunt G walked in front of us. We held each other hands to make sure no one got lost. When we boarded the train and got to our seats, we sat quietly while we rode. Finally arriving in Manhattan, I saw the tallest building I had ever seen. We rode in a big glass elevator all the way up to the 14th floor, to a beautiful spacious room with queen-sized beds. I felt like the rich and famous Aunt G was always talking about. I threw myself on the queen-sized bed and dreamt about being a movie star. "Hand me my drink. Where is my cigarette?" I laughed.

When Aunt G told us to get ready to go to the pool area, in my Marilyn Monroe's voice, I said to my sisters, "Come on girls. Let's go to the pool." When we arrived at the pool area, there were a few people. The pool area had been set up for the black employees' family members to enjoy. I got excited by everything that I saw. I jumped in the water in the deep end and started sinking to the bottom, forgetting that I could not swim. I began to sink, and I was so scared! I looked around and all I saw was water. I screamed on the inside, *help someone I'm drowning!* But no one could hear me. I was losing my breath and I felt a tearing and burning sensation in my chest as the water passed down my airway. I began to panic as I felt like I was going to die. I struggled to swim, but I couldn't. *God help me! I am about to die!*

I tried to swim, fighting against the water. I only got weaker and weaker. My heart was beating fast and I was crying. Just

135

when I was about to give up trying, I felt a strong hand reach and pull me out of the water. The life guard had jumped in the water to save me. He took me out of the water and placed me at the side of the pool. I was shaken, cold and scared. I looked around for sympathy from Aunt G and my sisters who were laughing until they could not laugh anymore. After I caught my breath, I laughed too.

"Ha-ha-ha! You thought you could swim in the deep end!" They hollered and laughed. Aunt G said, "I bet you stay yo' tail with us next time, Marilyn Monroe! Ha-ha-ha!" I expected Aunt G to fuss, but she just smirked.

After we left the pool area, we went to the hotel's restaurant. We were escorted by a maître d wearing an elegant tuxedo. He was a tall, handsome black man. He presented to us our fancy round table with white table cloths. I never saw anyone dressed like him before. I thought, *we are important today*. He had a napkin draped over his left arm and asked, "Would the ladies like to sit?" I got real fancy with my voice and said "Yes, we ladies would." The girls and Aunt G laughed at me, but I did not care. I felt fancy.

I sat down like Marilyn Monroe would. We sat down to eat our cheeseburgers, French fries and grape soda. Aunt G instructed us to use our fork and knife properly; she showed us how to cut our cheeseburger. "Do not pick up that damn cheeseburger with your hands," she said. Right away, I learned how to eat with a fork and knife.

On that day, I told myself that I was special. That day changed my life. I could be an important person and I was special. I knew from that day on that there was a different world where people were treated nicely. I had gone to a special place and it was beautiful. Thank you, Aunt G. We left that special place with joy and happiness. As we headed on the subway to return home, I was walking like royalty. No one may have noticed, but I did it anyway. I will always remember that day. Aunt G thought enough of us to take us out of the ghetto for a day to see a whole new world. I do not know the impression it made on my sisters, because we never talked about it. Going on that day trip gave me a whole new perspective on life. Everyone was not living like we were. Some people were happy. Somehow, it showed me that I could be anything and anyone I wanted to be.

Chapter 15
My Father

September 26, 1971 was my 12th birthday. My relatives said that at twelve years old, I acted like an old lady. "That child is old and mean. She does not talk much." In fact, I talked a lot; I just did not talk to them. They never had anything nice or important to say, so why should I talk to those old folks? In my mind, I talked all the time.

I never gave my birthday much thought. Most of my relatives did not have anything good to say to me on my birthday or any other day for that matter. One of my cousins, Sam Junior always gave me five dollars. Sam Junior was nice to us; the others gave nothing, no birthday cards, cake, money or happy birthday greetings. I suppose my birthday was not a happy event for anyone; no one acknowledged it. I promised myself that one day when I was able, I would plan to celebrate my own birthday. When I got a job and had money, I would celebrate like the world had never seen.

Aunt G let me know to her my birthday was just another day. I dismissed Aunt G and her crude remarks. In Aunt G's room, I looked in the mirror to try to tame my long coarse and thick deep brown unmanageable hair. My hair was down the middle of my back and I did not like it.

When I looked at myself, all I saw was a tall girl with skinny legs. My cousins always made fun of my long skinny legs. Singing some song about who wants the girl with the skinny legs? I supposed it was funny to them, but not to me. *Where did I get these skinny legs anyway? I don't know whether mama had skinny legs. I had never seen her legs.*

I had many thoughts running through my mind. I did more thinking than I did talking. I was a big dreamer, especially day dreaming. My day dreams were better than real life for me. I could escape to any place I wanted to, and I could do anything I wanted to do.

I loved being in Aunt G's bedroom; it was pretty and calm. It looked like one of those fancy bedrooms in the movies. I felt like I was in another world, and like I was someone else when I was there. No one else dared to come in; however, she knew that I went in her room and tried on her clothes and jewelry. Yet, she did not say anything. Besides, I slept with Aunt G mostly every night; that was probably why she did not say anything. Her bedroom was such a fun place for me. I rambled through her closet trying to figure out what to try on next. I wondered where she got all her beautiful clothes, hats, scarves, fur coats and pocketbooks.

I frequently looked in her mirror that was attached to a vintage, antique gray solid walnut dresser. Aunt G had a matching queen-sized bed with headboard. She got her furniture cheap, from one of her white folk employers and she always bragged about it. "I am not a riff-raff; I work. I work at one of the most important places in Manhattan and the people love me."

While in the midst of my daydreaming, I heard an unknown voice behind me. "Hey girl." I turned around and saw a tall, slim, handsome black man, with broad shoulders and a dark beard, hair trimmed neatly. His clothing fitted him very well and he had long skinny legs. I almost laughed, if it were not for the surprise seeing a man in Aunt G's bedroom. It was as if I had heard this voice before. It sounded so familiar; yet, I had never seen this man before. I moved slowly to look at the man when he spoke with such a smooth strong voice. I thought, *he better get out of here before Aunt G kills him!*

"Hi girl; I am your daddy," he said nonchalantly. My daddy!? My spirit leaped. I was overjoyed on the inside. *He had finally come to rescue me and take me away from here* were my immediate thoughts.

"My name is John."

"Hi John," I said without showing any emotion. What was

happening on the inside of my mind did not match to what I was saying on the outside. *Wait! He did not say happy birthday. Does he know that today is my birthday? Well, that does not matter; at least he is here. This is the best day of my life. John, my father is here to get me. I am going to take all my sisters with me. We are going to live happily ever after*! My spirit was jumping for joy.

"Come on girl," John said. We went down the stairs and outside. I wanted everyone outside to see that my daddy was there. I jumped into his big white Cadillac which was waiting outside for us. We rode for five miles and stopped at a big brown brick apartment complex. The neighborhood was much quieter than the one I lived in. Once we went inside the hallway, I saw long white and black marble floors. They were shiny and clean; I could almost see my reflection in the floors. My heart was beating fast. *Where are we going? Does he live here? Are we going to be living here together?*

The apartment we went into was on the first floor. We went inside and there were several people there waiting for us. He said, "Here she is. Vilma, this is your grandmother." *Grandmother?* I didn't understand.

She smiled at me and said, "You can call me Sarah." She was a petite woman, modestly dressed and very pretty with fair complexion. She almost looked white. She introduced me to some other people who were aunts and uncles. The other people spoke, but they did not seem happy to meet me. Some of them were even frowning when they looked at me.

I heard one of them ask my father, "Why did you bring her here Big John?" I felt someone staring at me and then I saw him. A young boy who looked exactly like my father and me coming out of a back room. John introduced us.

"Vilma, this is your brother, John Jr. He is eleven years old." I looked him up and down and smiled, but he did not smile back.

"Hi," he said with hesitation, as if he was not sure whether he should speak or not.

We stayed at John's mother's apartment for a few hours. Sarah cooked dinner for us. I ate baked chicken, rice, green beans, and golden-brown biscuits. She brought out a cake like I had never seen before. It was a pretty pineapple coconut cake with glistening white icing on it. She cut me a huge slice and when the moist buttery goodness hit my tongue, I moaned with each fork full. I could have eaten the whole cake. I wanted more but was too scared to ask for it. We had never had cake at home before.

That was by far the best day of my life. I never wanted to leave my new family. I could not wait to get back and tell the girls and especially Aunt G, who I found. *Ha-ha-ha! She would be*

143

surprised. She was the one who said that he did not want me. My mind was in a whirlwind. *The girls could live here with me.*

Just as I was about moved into my new home in my mind, Big John said, "Come on; let's go." He took me back home after that nice long visit. I was still filled with excitement about meeting him. He was nothing like Aunt G said. He was not a riff-raff or trifling, no-good man. He was John, my father. When John dropped me off home, he said, "Vilma, I will be back next Saturday at 5:00pm to pick you up." I said okay with a smile and jumped out of the car. I skipped all the way up the stairs.

"Yawl are not going to believe what happened today!" I told them how he came into Aunt G's bedroom, scooped me up into his arms and carried me to his car. I talked about how I met my grandmother Sarah, who was a sweet lady and my handsome brother John Jr. "I have a brother, Oh, yawl! They treated me like royalty and fed me the biggest and prettiest cake I have ever seen. That cake was so big; it could hardly fit on the table." Excited, they looked at me with their mouths wide open. "I think I am going to live with them. He promised to pick me to take me away next Saturday at 5:00pm.

"Do you think you will take us with you?" Shy asked. "Yes, I will. You can all go! Aunt G, my father came for me today." "Hmph; don't get your hopes up too high. He is still no good.

What is he coming here for now?"

"No, Aunt G; you don't understand. He came for me! Today!"

"I heard you. Now go and sit down somewhere."

She did not understand, but she would when he took me from here. The next week, all I did was daydream, about what John and I would do when he came to get me. All I could think about that week was John, and when he was arriving to get me. The excitement of it all, was sometimes more than I could stand. I talked about it all week and Aunt G got tired of me talking. The girls loved hearing about the tasty food, the new relatives and us leaving to go to our new home.

Saturday had finally arrived, and I was ready at 3:00pm. I wore my best outfit, a white and blue dress with my best shoes. I combed my hair into two ponytails, with a blue ribbon on each ponytail. I ran down the stairs and said goodbye to the girls. "I will see you all later!" Aunt G did not say a word, but I did not care; I was going with John.

I sat on the stoop and waited. Each time I saw a big white car, I stood up. I sat on the stoop for two hours, excited that finally, five o'clock came. I thought John was going to be pulling up at any moment, in that big white Cadillac. I waited and watched the cars passing. I even walked up the street, searching in cased I missed his car.

Six o'clock in the evening, and no John. Eight o'clock, still no John. My heart was hurting, and my head was spinning. I was confused and crying on the inside, yet I still had hope that he would come and get me. I thought, *something bad must have happened to him. He must be sick or working*. I felt so bad; I could hardly hold my head up. Still, I continued to look up the street, searching for his car. There was no sign of John anywhere. *He would not forget me; I am his daughter*.

Aunt G yelled at me, "Get in here and eat! He is not coming, stupid girl. I told you he was no good. Do not depend on a man to keep his word. Eat your food!" I ate without tasting the food. My mind was confused. *Where was he?* I kept looking out of the window for John to show up, but he did not.

Two weeks later, I heard someone blowing a car horn outside. I looked out of the window and it was John! I shouted with glee, "Aunt G! He is here to get me!" I ran to gather my things and go, but she did not say a word. I ran and jumped in the car.

"Hi girl."

"Hi John!" John Jr. was in the car and he spoke and smiled. He was so handsome and dressed very well with a similar haircut to John's. We got to Sarah's house and ate some tasty food. John Jr. and I got along as if we had known each other our whole lives. The other relatives looked at me as if I was an alien. They made me feel uncomfortable. As they whispered, I listened carefully. One of them came to me and gave me five dollars. "Thank you, I said. But as I left the room to go to the bathroom, I saw the same person give John Jr. money.

"Do not tell her that I gave you ten dollars. You are better than her; she gets five. You are Big John's legitimate child and she is not. John Jr. responded, "She is pretty." The relative came back, "But you are more handsome."

My heart sank about what I heard and saw. I tried to put it in the back of my mind as I held my five dollars in my hand. I went into the living room and sat down in a chair. John left me there with John Jr. and Sarah. He showed up hours later and said, "Come on." He took me back to Aunt G's and said, "I will be back for you next Saturday at five; okay?"

"Okay, John!"

This time, John returned as he said. I was with my father most weekends after that. I left Aunt G's most of the time without saying good-bye to anyone. I returned when I wanted to. I had begun to take my sisters with me as I promised. Every time I went to visit John, I had one of them with me. I mostly took Shy with me. This went on for three years.

Chapter 16

Waiting

At the age of fifteen, I enjoyed living with my father, Big John, and his girlfriend Jessica. They had not asked me to live with them; I took it upon myself to move in. I moved my clothes in a little at a time, unnoticed by them. I invited my sister Shy along with me. The other sisters did not want to join us at Big John's house.

"Sit down on the couch Vilma," Big John's said with a serious look on his face. "You cannot continue to keep bringing Shy with you. I cannot feed both of you. She is not my daughter." Those words hurt my feelings. I did not want to lose John now that we have found each other. So, I took Shy back home. I felt bad, but there was nothing I could do about it. I could not bear the thought of telling her that she was not wanted at John's house either. I did not tell her she could not return with me; I just did not bring her back. I packed the rest of my clothes at Aunt G's and left for good. I did not say goodbye to anyone. Goodbyes were too painful for me. It was easier just to leave.

I was happy to finally have a home in a normal environment, with a mother and father. Jessica, John's teenage girlfriend was only three years older than me; she was eighteen years old. She was not happy with the living arrangements and was jealous of our relationship. She liked bossing me around and she was mean.

I ignored her as much as possible. She demanded me to clean the house and mop the floor. I thought when she spoke, *please shut up*. But John agreed with her. *He was gone most of the time, what did he know.* It was mainly Jessica and I in the apartment and she kept the apartment spic and span by making me mop on my hands and knees, with bleach and water like I was her maid. I got tired of her telling me what to do.

I was afraid of her, so I did what she wanted. Her five feet eight inches stature made her intimidating. Her slim figure weighed in at one hundred and twenty pounds. She was a perfect size seven and dressed like a movie star. I hated those big thick glasses she wore though. They made her eyeballs huge, with her crossed eyes. She could see nothing without those big thick glasses. She wore wigs that looked good on her and her makeup was perfect, even though she wore too much for my taste. She loved smoking cigarettes. The way she held her cigarettes in her hand looked sophisticated, while she drank her rum and coke. The rumor among my father's people, was that she was seventeen years old, even though she looked thirty. They said she ran away from home to be with Big John.

150

I tried to get along with her because I did not want to go back to Aunt G's. I liked living with my father. I went to school from John's house. I changed my school district again without telling Aunt G. I also changed my name at school to John's last name, Cook. I was now Vilma Cook.

Jessica and John fought all the time, about him coming home late. John did not act like he wanted to be with her; I believe that made her sad. When he arrived home late, he always brought me Chinese food. Often, I ate the Chinese food, not remembering I ate it.

Aunt G said that when I was younger, I would sleep walk. One night I was sleep walking and almost walked out of the window three stories up. "Fool get out of the window before you fall!" Aunt G screamed loudly. I woke up and saw that I had one foot out of the window.

John asked me the next day if I liked the Chinese food he brought in the night before. I told him that I did never remember eating it. He said, "You ate it like you were hungry. You also cleaned up the kitchen when you finished." I laughed and walked away. I could smell the aroma from the Chinese food the next day. So I must have been sleep walking, sleep eating and sleep cleaning!

Jessica and I began spending more time together as John

disappeared. She was starting to grow on me. Jessica and I went out shopping together. One day, she was in a good mood because she had just gotten paid. I believed she liked pretending to be a mother as well. We shopped at a local store on Broadway that sold dresses for only five dollars. She bought me three dresses she picked out for me. I did not like them, but I did not say anything. I just wore the ugly dresses. When we got back to the apartment, John still was not there. Jessica cooked dinner which was chicken and dumplings. I dared not tell her that I hated those mushy biscuits and chicken mixed up together. I stomached as much as I could eat. She was not a good cook, unlike my Aunt G, who was an excellent cook. But, it was better than no food at all. After dinner, I cleaned the dishes and kitchen. Then, we prepared for bed.

Startled by strange noises and not being able to breathe, I woke up out of my sleep! I jumped up from the bed, choking from my room being filled with smoke. Something was burning! I could hear screaming going on next door. My room was at the end of the apartment in the back with a small window, that I kept open for air. My room was close to the apartment next door and I spent a lot of time hanging out of my window, talking to the girl next door.

My stomach began to feel sick from the smoke. I heard fire engines along with crackling and popping sounds of sparks from the raging fire. Then panic hit my brain. I could not think straight and was unable to see due to the smoke. I ran to the other side of the apartment in a panic looking for John and Jessica. I remember thinking that they must be outside already. *Why did they leave me?*! I screamed for help, but no sound came out of my mouth. My heart felt like it was going to explode out of my chest. I was unable to breathe. *Be still; don't move*, I heard in my head. I didn't know what to do. I was so scared, and no one was home with me! I opened all the windows in the apartment to get fresh air. When I opened the windows, the apartment filled with more smoke. I heard all the commotion outside; people crying, and glass breaking. The crackle of the fire was loud as it burned the building next door to the ground.

The continuous sound of bricks falling next door made me jump. Then I saw chairs flying past my window. The firemen were tossing out burning furniture. I heard parts of the building crash to the ground, but I was too afraid to move. I did not even want anyone to know that I was home. The firemen had evacuated the building that I was in, but the fire was contained next door. The building was destroyed, but I did not want to go back to Aunt G's. When the firemen knocked on the door, I did not answer. Exhausted with fear, I sat in the living room chair and cried myself asleep.

The next morning, Jessica returned. She looked sad, but that was because we had not heard from my father in two weeks.

John was not nice to Jessica; when he was home, he fought with her. He stayed out overnight often. Jessica said nothing about the fire, nor did she ask if I was okay. I did not care about Jessica's feelings and she did not care about mine. We got dressed and I went to school smelling like smoke. Jessica left for work; no words came out of her mouth or mine. There was no hello or goodbye. I had a dreadful day at school, smelling like smoke. No one made any comments about it though. I supposed they heard about the fire. I returned home from school. My room still smelled like smoke, and so did I.

I had not seen John in two weeks. Jessica and I pretended like everything was normal. We woke up; she went to work, and I went to school. We did not speak to each other. She cooked, and I cleaned.

Jessica left for work earlier than usual the next day. I thought, *Good! I don't have to look at her. John will be back soon. I will tell him about her nasty ways, and how bad she treated me. He will not like that at all. Everything will be back to normal. He will bring me some good Chinese food again.*

I ate breakfast at a restaurant on the way to school of biscuits with cheese and jelly. I returned home from school, but no one was there. No John, no Jessica. But, I did not give it much thought. The lady who lived on the first floor brought her five-year-old daughter upstairs to our apartment because she wanted me to comb her daughter's hair. Her daughter's hair was long like mine, but I did not want to comb that long thick hair. The neighbor offered me five dollars to comb her hair. I needed some money for food, so I agreed.

It took me two hours to comb and braid her hair. Afterwards I went the grocery store to buy food to cook for dinner. I ate, watched television until I was tired and went to bed. Two days later and still no John or Jessica. Each time I looked out the window for John, tears rolled down my face. I begged in my mind, *Lord please let John come back*. I began to feel lost and rejected again. I wondered where he was and what he was doing. I was thinking that something bad had happened to John. I believed he would be back soon and I waited for him. Two weeks passed, and I realized after a while that they were not returning. I showed no emotions as I packed my bags and headed back to Aunt G's.

I walked back home, and it took me two hours. The doors at Aunt G's were never locked; it was as if she knew that I would be returning. I walked in the house, put my clothes up and got something to eat. My sisters did not speak to me. They did not show any emotions toward me returning. No sadness or happiness, they were still in a *fog* just like me. I supposed all that we had been through had shown us that emotions do not help an unpleasant situation.

Aunt G returned home from work. I was so nervous, as I waited for her to say something sarcastic. She did not fail me. "Hmph! He left your behind, didn't he? Now you come running back here. I was waiting for you; I knew it would happen. He left Charity, your mother the same way. That man is no good; he will never be any good. You should have stayed your butt here. But noooo! You had to see for yourself! Going to live with my father," she smirked. "See what your father did for you?" She looked at me and said, "See, now don't you? What a trifling no-good bum he is. Damn! When will you ever learn? Ha-ha-ha! He-he-he!" She laughed and took a swig of her rum and coke, then she swirled her finger in the ice. She strutted off smiling as if she had just won the first prize of being right.

My thoughts were screaming in my head. *I bet I will never trust him again! He has left me too many times! I cannot wait until I can get out of this house for good!* I went back to my own room; I did not sleep with Aunt G anymore from that day on.

Chapter 17

Fifteen

I hated being fifteen! Can't do this and can't do that! You too big to be acting like that, too old to act like that! You are not old enough for that! What was I supposed to do? Ugh! Aunt G got on my nerves more as I got older.

High school was my escape from the chaos at home. I joined the dance team, the gymnastics team, and the drama class. I loved dance class the most. The best dancer in the class was Sofia. She was a fifteen-year-old pretty Latina girl. She had long curly black hair with tanned brown skin. She danced with ease and pose and moved effortlessly. I watched her petite body move all around the dance floor like a ballerina. I was jealous of her and how the boys paid attention to her and not me.

I was tall and clumsy. I did not look right dancing, even though I loved it. I worked hard at dancing and gymnastics. I did good at gymnastics and my coach Ms. Guruwhich, was nice. She was a tall slender German lady in her late thirties. She spoke in a low soft-toned voice while she smiled. She told me that "I could be whatever I wanted to be in life." She said that "everyone was not meant to be the same. You are beautiful and smart. You must believe in yourself." That was nice of her, because I had no faith or confidence in myself.

When I danced, I forgot all about my problems at home. Once I gained my confidence, I became one of the best dancers on the floor. I looked good on the floor during the gymnastic meets as well. I combined dance and tumbling. I would get so excited when it was my time on the floor. "Take a deep breath," Ms. Guruwhich said. I took a deep breath and hit the floor. I felt good, all the people watching and waiting to see what I would do. I was on point too. My routine was flawless, as I flowed through the air. When my routine was over, I received a score of seven points. I had done great! We won the match and I had helped. Miss Guruwhich looked at me and smiled. "I told you, you could do it! Congratulations!" I smiled all the way home. That was one of the best gymnastic meets our team ever had that year.

I never invited anyone from home to the meets. That part of my life was just for me. Besides, I did not want anyone to see how they behaved. They would embarrass me anyway. When I got home that evening from our team winning the match, I said, "Look Aunt G! I got a trophy in gymnastics!" I handed the trophy to her. She took it, looked it over, smiled and said, "That's good." She reached into her dress pocket and pulled out at key. She opened her china cabinet, where she displayed her valuable pieces of china. She put my trophy right in front in the china cabinet and walked away. She did not know but that was one of the happiest moments I ever had with her. A few words were spoken, but I knew she approved.

I had a great school year and I was looking forward to my future changing. The end of the school year came and went. I was ready to hang out with my favorite cousin, Cheryl. I had not seen her for a few months, since I was busy with school, while Cheryl was in her apartment, drinking most of the time. My cousin Cheryl was wild. We rode in cabs together, but when it was time to pay the cab driver Cheryl would yell, "Jump out now!" She jumped out of the cab first and I jumped after she did. We ran as fast as we could, laughing all the way home. The furious cab driver drove fast, trying to catch us. We ran through apartment buildings and the cab driver was unable to catch us. Cheryl was loads of fun and I loved her. She was twenty-five years old, ten years older than me. Yet, she treated me like I was her equal and mattered to her, except when she had a hangover. She did not want to be bothered with me or anyone else at that time.

Cheryl always had lots of men in her apartment. There were times, I had gone downstairs to her apartment and the men were laying around drunk and sleep. I would go to her refrigerator and get what I wanted to eat. Her doors were usually unlocked. No one locked their doors in the building.

People always talked about how dangerous Brooklyn was, but we had no fear. We had Aunt G!

Cheryl's bad moods, normally came from Aunt G cursing her out, combined with her drunken hangovers. Aunt G often told her that "she was a no-good drunk on welfare." My heart would hurt when Aunt G said that she "wished her daughter Cheryl was never born."

"Why can't you be like your sister? She is married with a beautiful family and a magnificent home. Makes me sick just to look at you. I felt like killing myself to think that I gave birth to something like you. Look at this place! It is a mess just like you!"

After that horrible encounter with Aunt G, Cheryl locked her door for days. No one could get through, including me. I banged on her door ensuring that it was me. "Get away from here!" she responded. "Stop banging on my door! Go away!" I wanted to ensure Cheryl that someone was on her side, that she was not alone. But I could not get through. I held my head down and headed back upstairs, upset with Cheryl. I enjoyed my summers with friends and sisters. I was two days away from being sixteen and I wanted to do something special on my birthday.

Chapter 18

Sweet Sixteen

Waking up early on my birthday, the sun was bright, stung my eyes. I heard people say when you turn sixteen, it is a fun time, and you're almost grown. My main objective was to get out of Aunt G's house when high school was over. I planned to go off to college.

Aunt G gave me some birthday money and I took the subway to Manhattan to shop at Macy's. I bought a sexy outfit for my sweet sixteen birthday. I planned to wear that outfit and parade up and down the street showing it off.

When I returned home, I saw my cousin Junior and Cook. I was excited to see them because they always gave me and my sisters money for our birthdays. My cousins were nice and loads of fun. They talked funny with a combined Jamaican and South Carolinian accents. People called it the "Geechie" accent. I practiced not talking like that after the kids on the block made fun of me. Aunt G's accent was so strong that people had a tough time understanding her. When Aunt G fussed at my cousins, they did not pay any mind to her. They said, "Be quiet G. You fuss to darn much. Get the liquor and let's have a drink."

They all sat down to drink, laughing and having fun.

Aunt G called me, "Vilma go down to the basement and find where I hid my good Jamaican rum. You know where I put it." I loved going down to the basement because Aunt G allowed me to decorate the basement in psychedelic colors. I had strobe lights of assorted colors on cords all over the basement. Sometimes our local rock band came through to practice in our basement and I loved it. They were all cute, so all the girls on the block got jealous. I did not let any of the girls I did not like in the basement when the band was playing. I saved that special time for my friends and myself.

I made my way to the basement, turned on the light switch and people were everywhere yelling, "Surprise!! Happy Sweet Sixteen!!" Cheryl gave me a big hug and kissed my cheek. "Girl, I love you! Happy sweet sixteen!" Cheryl had planned and given me a surprise party. I was smiling as the tears rolled down my face.

"You can drink some beer tonight," Cheryl whispered with a sly smile. As I scanned the room, I saw a big cake on the counter that read "Happy Sweet Sixteen Vilma." There was beer on the counter as well. I was totally surprised. My cousin Cheryl was smiling at me with a look of love on her face. No one had ever had good thoughts concerning me like Cousin Cheryl. I felt so special. I wore my special outfit I purchased from Macy's. It was a Pocahontas skirt outfit; the top was plunged deep with cleavage peeping through, with beige and black fringes. The beige skirt was fitting my little round hips tight with fringes at the bottom as well. I was looking good, even if I have to say so myself.

I walked over to where the cake was, as the song "Family Affair" played on the record player. I danced with my friends until I could not dance anymore. I took my very first drink in the basement that day, rum spiked with red punch. The music was loud, but Aunt G stayed away. We laughed, partied and was having fun.

One of my friends, called me in a corner. He was holding a lit marijuana joint between his fingers. "You are sixteen now," he said. Hit this." I took the marijuana out of his fingers and took a small puff. "Suck it in girl; hit it." I took a longer draw on that long white paper stick that looked like a cigarette. I pulled hard on that joint a few times. I drank some more spiked punch and danced. I became dizzy and sick within a few minutes. I felt the room spinning around. I got dizzy and passed out. The next thing I remembered, I was being carried up the basement stairs by my two cousins Bee and Samey. Samey had my arms and Bee had my legs. I heard Cheryl asking, as they carried me up the steep stairs, "What happened to her?"

"I guess she is a drunk sweet sixteen," they laughed. "She

cannot hold her liquor." I could not move or speak. I tried to speak but the words did come out. I could hear voices talking. "Be careful; do not hit her head on the wall." I could hear Cheryl's voice, which gave me comfort. They took me to my room and laid me down. I woke up the next day, with a pounding headache. Aunt G was standing over me holding a glass with some yellow slimy stuff in it. "Drink this you riff-raff. Don't know how to hold your liquor." She handed me the glass and it had two raw eggs in it with liquid. I did not want to drink it, but Aunt G insisted. I drank the mixture and to my surprise, I felt better. I decided to visit my brother John, since he was not at my birthday party. One thing about my brother, if it was not about him, he was not interested. He lived just two blocks away from me.

When I arrived at John's apartment building, there were two boys standing in the doorway. One of them spoke to me, but I did not speak back. The tall dark-skinned boy was named Buck. I did not want any attention from him because I heard that he was bad. He was two weeks out of prison, for serial rape. The other boy was Toby, a fat college boy with a big belly. He was follower and easily persuaded by Buck. Upon passing them in the doorway, I felt a strange feeling in my stomach like butterflies. I had to pass them to get upstairs where my brother John lived. They were blocking the door way, so I had to step over them. They smiled at each other, looked like they were up to no good.

Buck spoke to me again. Nervously I spoke under my breath, "Hey."

"What you can't speak? Do you think you are too good to talk girl?"

I moved passed them cautiously and slowly. I made my way past them in the hallway. My right foot barely touched the first step, towards where my brother lived. I felt someone grab me from behind. I was thrown over the big broad shoulders of Buck, like I was a doll. My head faced downward with my hips on his shoulder. He carried me up a flight of stairs, as my mind raced with fear. I felt and heard my heart beating fast, in my chest. Buck got me to the top of the stairs and kicked open an apartment door that was not locked. It was as if they were waiting for me to walk through the front door. There was a large bed placed in the middle of the floor, with a beige bedspread. Buck threw me off his shoulders and I bounced on the bed, scared to death.

"What are you doing man?!" Toby shouted nervously. "I thought you were kidding when you said let's grab her."

"Shut up Toby! What did you think we were doing here? We going to get some sweet tail. I bet she's a virgin. Do you want to go first Toby? Since you are still a virgin too," he laughed.

"You want me to show you how it is done first?"

Toby said, "I am not for this. You just got out of jail for a rape charge."

"She came looking for it," Buck said. "Look at her! She wants it bad."

"I am not trying to catch a charge, Buck!" Toby screamed, "You better stop!"

"Come on man, she's yours. Have some fun with her." Buck looked at Toby with a glare in his eyes that scared me. Then I heard him say, "We can get rid of her and no one will ever know. We can have a good time," he smiled.

"No, no, no!" Toby's voice trembled in fear. He began to panic, looking around the room for an escape route for himself. He was afraid of Buck; everyone in the neighbor was. He had a reputation for hurting people. Buck stayed in jail for raping women, beating men, and robbing homes.

"I am not doing it. Stop!" yelled Toby.

"Shut up Toby!" Buck screamed back.

I was scared out of my mind, as I looked back and forth at them arguing over what to do with me. I tried to move, but I was frozen still. I tried to scream, no words came out of my mouth.

166

My heart was beating faster though my chest. My little short skirt was pulled up over my waist. My legs were up in the air, being held by Buck with one hand. I did not think about pulling away or even fixing my skirt. Fear had gripped me. I was afraid that they would hear my heart beating fast and hurt me. Then, I heard the best words I have ever heard in my life. "Get out of here girl!" I snatched my legs from Buck, jumped up as fast as I could. "You better not tell anybody, or I will kill you," Buck threatened me. "You hear me?" I shook my head yes, because I still could not speak.

I ran as fast as I could up the stairs to my brother, John's apartment. I did not say anything to John or his mother. I dismissed the whole ordeal out of my mind. I found out months later that Buck was arrested on murder and rape charges. Buck was sentenced to twenty years in jail. I was secretly happy, because it meant that I did not have to see him ever. I could have been the one killed instead of the poor woman he murdered. So, I kept my secret.

I was glad when it was time to go back to school. I was surprised when I was chosen to go to a school out of my neighborhood. I was told it was for a better education.

Chapter 19

Last Year of School

I was bussed to a school in Shepshed Bay, two hours from home. I had to get up at four am, to stand in the dark alone at a bus stop to be picked up by five am. I was one of several black children who were chosen to attend schools out of their districts. That was a lonely time for me. None of the other students at my new school spoke to me. They were told not to be rude, just do not speak. After staying there for three months, one day I decided to sign myself out of that school and I never looked back.

I loved high school in my own neighborhood. I did not fit in at the other school. My cousins and the children at school, said I looked mean. They said I always had a frown on my face and behaved strangely. I was quiet and did not talk much. I stared into space all the time, talking in my own head. I did not pay attention to people. I stayed in a *fog* and held my feelings in all the time.

My daydreaming all the time caused me not to have many friends. My only real friend was John Jr. He attended schools for smarter kids and I forged my school papers to follow John.

His mother switched his schools often. I believed to get him away from me. Whatever schools he went to, I wanted to go as well. I worked as hard as I could, so that I would be accepted in the schools he attended. My strategy worked for a while; Aunt G did not care what school I attended if I did not bother her.

John's mother did everything in her power to make sure that we were separated. His mother did not like me, but I understood why. My mother dated her husband, when they were young teenagers. My mother did not know my father was married. John's mother talked bad to me, called me names and told me I was ugly. She told me one day that God made a mistake when He put me together. She would often remind me that she had one child and did not need other one coming around. She told me that "my mother was not a good a mother and she was a tramp." I never said anything back to her; she reminded me of Aunt G in some ways. The way her words could hurt to your core was exactly like Aunt G. I told Aunt G once what John's mother was saying to me. Aunt G went to her house and cursed her out. They had a time cursing at each other, neither of them backed down.

When I went back to Thomas Jefferson High School, John's mother allowed him to go as well. We were two of the most popular people in high school. The girls hated me because the boys loved me. The boys thought that I was cute, even though they did not try to date me. They may have been afraid of John. The girls loved John Jr. They said he was fine to look at. He looked just like our father Big John to me. He was tall slender built, with dark smooth skin. He had beautiful large round eyes that sparkled. John did not date any of the girls in school. He was in love with one girl in the neighborhood and had plans to marry her when he got out of high school. I was not interested in the boys at school; they were too silly for me to date. I had too many things to do to pay attention to boys. My dancing, gymnastics and drama clubs kept me busy.

I was afraid of boys. Aunt G said, "If any of you come home pregnant, you have to leave my house. I am not taking care of no babies. I can hardly feed you all, talking about a baby. If boys looked you the wrong way, you get pregnant. Look at your Mother! Men never did her any good." I needed to get Aunt G out of my head.

Our neighborhood marijuana dealer Slicky was 21 years old, He sold his drugs at high schools. He hung out with my brother John and I when he visited. Slicky gave us free marijuana in hopes of getting us hooked on the drug. We smoked it during school hours. John would give me a signal to leave English class. Laughing, we would go out, behind the staircase to meet Slicky and smoke our joint. He lit the joint and passed it to John. John would take a puff and pass it to me, with instructions on how to do it correctly. I smoked, coughed, choked and we all laughed.

I felt good, as a sensation of warmth hit my head. We ran back in class, laughing at everything the teacher said. Every time we went out to smoke marijuana, we disrupted class with our laughter. The teacher frowned at us, showing her wrinkles at the top of her forehead. I saw her mouth move, as she whispered, "Stop it," under her breath. The whole class watched as John and I laughed. I laughed so hard tears rolled down my face. My stomach was hurting from using my laughing muscles. When I laughed I held nothing back, I laughed from my heart. It was good to laugh, it took away the pain, of being at home.

We were eventually put out of the classroom. I was glad, because she put us out at lunch time. We had the munchies. John and I went to the teacher's lounge, pretending that we were student teachers. The teacher's lounge had a large variety of foods. We ordered our food; I ordered a ham and cheese sandwich with lettuce, tomatoes on bagel, with chips, and a Hershey candy bar. John ordered pepperoni pizza and a Mr. Good bar. We sat down and ate with the teachers. No one noticed that we were not teachers. We behaved with sophistication, whispering among ourselves. After we ate, we giggled and went back to class.

I had on a long flowing checkered skirt and a white blouse that

172

I made. I loved sewing class and made most of my clothes. I made my skirt out of Aunt G's curtains earlier that morning. I waited for her to leave for work and took the curtains right off her windows. I did not do anything major, just a basic base stitching. John Jr. had on his black suit with a white shirt and tie. We loved dressing up like movie stars we saw on television. When I got home, I was able to unravel the stitch from my skirt and hung the curtains right back up before she noticed.

John was a good student. He passed his classes with all A's. John wanted to be a doctor, and me, well I was not as smart as John. I studied hard to pass with a B or C. But my plan was to go to college and become a social worker. Aunt G thought I was smart. "You are smart Vilma, but you do not have any common sense."

During our senior year in school, John, my brother, disappeared again. I did not know where my brother was nor did I try to find out; I focused on finishing high school. I decided to finish my last year at Thomas Jefferson High school. I made sure that I went home each day to complete my homework and study.

One day after my math class, my teacher Mr. Carter told me to stay after class. I wonder what he wanted. He was always nice to me. "Vilma," he said with a concerned look on his face, "You are not passing math. If you do not pass math, you will not be able to graduate with your class. It would be a shame for a smart girl like you not to pass."

I looked at him with a sad expression. "I must graduate. I need to go to college and get away from Brooklyn."

"I will help you." Then he gave me a concerned look. "I will tutor you once a week, so you can pass this class."

"Thank you, Mr. Carter," I said without showing my excitement.

Chapter 20
Graduation Day

F inally, it was my graduation day and I was excited. I did not tell Aunt G, or my sisters the date of my graduation. I did not want anyone to embarrass me. Aunt G was loud and had a way of upsetting any atmosphere with her accusations and loud mouth. Besides, I did not need anyone.

Thomas Jefferson High School officials did not think enough of students to give us a proper prom, like everyone else had. Therefore, I planned to wear my prom dress on graduation day. I bought a new dress from Macy's for the ceremony. It was a long, flowing silk emerald green gown, with a split on the left side that started from the top of my thigh and went all the way down my long legs. The front of the dress had a slight plunge in the front, fitting tightly around my firm breasts. The dress hit and held my body in all the right places to show off everything. The clerk in Macy's questioned me about my dress choice for graduation and did not approve. "Are you sure you want to wear that dress on the day of your graduation?"

"Yes," I smirked. *I love to shock people,* I said in my mind.

I applied my own makeup, and I was good at it. I wore makeup all the time to disguise my bad acne scars. I styled my hair and I thought I was looking good. I admired my appearance, as I looked in the mirror. I was proud of my size six, and measurements of thirty-six, twenty-four, and thirty-six. I had the same measurements as Marilyn Monroe and worked hard at keeping my Marilyn Monroe figure.

On the way to graduation, I stood at the bus stop peaceful. I was happy and proud to have completed the task of high school. No one in my family had finished school. Most of them dropped out in middle school. Adorned in my outfit and cap, I admired my cap with its navy and orange trim, and held my gown over my arm.

I knew I would not miss my overcrowded school. We were the forgotten school and no one cared if we graduated or not. Yet, I was grateful for the teachers who cared. My gymnastics and math teachers were dear to me. I will never forget their kindness and patience towards me. As I waited for the bus, I was thinking about the rumor that my school was scheduled to close for good, due to the sparse number of graduates. That did not sit well with me on graduation day.

Finally, I was at school. The ceremony had started and the auditorium was packed with well-wishers, those happy to see their family members graduate. As for me, I did not have any supporters. My name was called for my diploma, "Vilma Jones." I walked across that stage smiling, even though no one was yelling my name, like I heard when the other students stood to get their diploma.

I got up from my seat excited and strutted to the stage like Marilyn Monroe would. I walked up the small flight of stairs. The principal smiled at me and reached out his hand to shake mine. He had my high school diploma in his hand. I extended my hand, and shook his as I received my diploma.

As I extended my hand to receive my diploma, I heard voices of my past saying to me, "You will never finish high school. You will be pregnant with five kids before you are fifteen. You will never amount to anything or be anyone important." But here I was at the proudest moment of my life, receiving my high school diploma. Not only did I earn my diploma, I was the first one in my family to graduate from high school. Yet there was no one to see it.

I heard the applause as I walked proudly across the stage to get my diploma. My cap and gown swaying. When the principal put that diploma in my hand, he put my freedom in my hand. I took a deep breath, as I smiled to reach for that piece of paper that said, "Well done." A profound sense of freedom and accomplishment hit me. Tears welled up in my eyes; I was ready for my fresh start.

Also, I received a reward in gymnastics. I could not wait to show Aunt G. I knew she would be proud of me. At the end of the ceremony, we all turned our tassels to the left and it was over! On my way outside, I was smiling and happy. I watched as other graduates hugged their families who were proud of them as well.

"Vilma!" I heard someone calling my name with excitement. I turned around to see who it was, and it was my step brother's mother. I thought, *what a pleasant surprise.* "Where is John?" I asked. Seeing her should have been a good thing, but normally it was not. She had disdain for me that was unnerving.

She found ways to cut with her words just like Aunt G. They hated each other, yet they were alike in many ways. For one they were both mean. Whenever Aunt G saw John's mother, she told her that John, Sr. was no good. She reminded her how he went after my mother to get her pregnant even though he knew that he was married to her. She told John's mother the story on how he went to court to deny me and wanted to pay that small amount of child support. Aunt G would scream, "I told him to stick that little money where the sun doesn't shine."

John's mother gave it right back to Aunt G. "That's right! He is married to me, and we have only one child! John Jr. is his real child. Everyone else has five or more children with no father for the children." They argued each time they saw each other. They told the same stories over and over to each other. Now she was at my graduation, one of the happiest days of my life.

"Hi Vilma," she said with a smug look on her face." I came to receive John's diploma." She was bragging as usual. "He is already in college. He graduated a year early. He is so smart."

What is she talking about? I thought. John graduated last year, when he was supposed to; that was not a year early. Who does she think she is fooling? Did she come to spoil my day? She was always trying to hurt me with her degrading words. It just gave her pleasure to hurt people with her words. You could see her smiling as she bragged about John Jr. She lived through his life because she had none of her own.

John Jr's mother continued with her negativity at my graduation celebration. "Your mother had five children with no husband. I had one great child, John Jr." I looked at her and said to myself, *enough of this crazy woman. I must get away from her.*

I smiled at her, stayed for a few minutes then left her standing there talking. I was not going to let her ruin my day. What a wonderful day it was! I ran into the house looking for Aunt G. "Look I graduated!" I shouted and smiled. I felt great and she was proud of me even though she did not say it. The expression on her face said it all. She was smiling, not like everyone else though; no teeth were showing.

"Aunt G," I explained with my jubilant voice, "I got accepted to Danbury Connecticut College." I knew she would be happy for me. I could leave for the next semester in August which was only three months away. Suddenly, the atmosphere in the room changed from light and happy to ugly and dark. I saw the *fog* fill the room. She started talking like she was a demon on television.

"Who do you think you are talking about college? Who do you think is going to pay for you to go to college Miss Thing? I don't have no money for college. Go and sit down somewhere...college!" She laughed. I could not believe she laughed at the word "college," with such an evil laugh. She snickered as if I had cursed at her or said something so ridiculous that all she could do was laugh.

No one in my family had finished high school and certainly not thought about going to college. It was unbelievable to her that I would think such a way. I stood there for a few minutes not sure of what to do next. I was in complete shock, and disbelief to her reaction. I thought she would have been happy that I wanted to go to college. I knew that she had the money. She often said that I was school smart, not common-sense smart.

It felt like she took a knife and stabbed me in my heart, pulled it out and dropped it on the floor. As I stood there trying to think, my head became foggy and light. I felt extremely faint.

I walked away as Aunt G stood looking out the window, with her back turned facing me as she dismissed me from her presence. I went to my room crying. *Think Vilma, what are you going to do?* The guidance counselor told me about a local college that would give me money to go to school to be a secretary. So, I settled for attending the local college in Manhattan and registered for the fall semester.

Chapter 21

A New Love

I got over the whole going away to college ordeal right away when I started attending the local college in Manhattan. School was out for the summer and I put my energy into partying in the clubs in Manhattan. I began hanging out with a college student, Lenora, who was my next-door neighbor. Soon we became friends.

Lenora was the only one in our neighborhood besides me who had attended college. Most people in our neighbor dropped out of high school. Lenora knocked on my door one day and invited me to go with her and her older friends to the hottest club in Manhattan. I was a freshman in community college and they were seniors at a four-year college. I was honored that she wanted me to hang out with her.

To me, Lenora was a quiet, sweet, twenty-one-year-old worldly mature woman. She was described by the people in the neighborhood as an old fashioned, beautiful, light-skinned girl. She dressed modest, unlike me. I loved wearing tight fitting dresses. Lenora had a beautiful shape, large plump tight butt, and a small waist. She was five feet two inches in height. It seemed to me that boys loved light skinned girls. I had a challenging time due to being tall and skinny.

Lenora frequented high-end clubs in Manhattan. I was with her one night and the bouncer decided who got in and who did not. When Lenora arrived at the club, the bouncer tipped his head, bowed, stepped aside, and let her in. Of course, I went right along with her.

At the time, she was dating a musician who worked at some of the clubs. The women liked him and wanted to be with him. When he was with Lenora, the women tried to get his attention. I wondered myself why he was with her. Lenora was a quiet person and did not speak much. When she did talk, it was with sophistication and good diction.

In our neighborhood, most of the girls on the block did not like her. They said that she was stuck up and she thought she was cute. I liked her a lot; she was my inspiration to do better in life. Lenora did not care what they whispered about her. She had two popular drug dealer brothers, Shorty and Lennie. Lenora's brothers kept her busy trying to keep them out of jail, and out of fights with other drug dealers. She didn't get any help from her mother though, since was a depressed alcoholic.

I found out a lot of information about them through my sister De-De, who dated Shorty. At the time, both of them were sixteen years old and it was obvious to all who saw them that they were in love. De-De and Shorty were inseparable. When you saw the one, you saw the other. De-De was happy being with him and said he took care of her and made her laugh. I loved watching those two short people walk up and down the street together, holding hands.

Unfortunately, De-De's happiness with Shorty was short-lived. Someone walked up to Shorty in broad day light and shot him. The rumor was that he was killed by rival drug dealers. The person looked him right in the eyes, smiled and shot him five times in the chest. That was the first murder that I remembered in my neighborhood. Shorty laid dead in the middle of the street for the whole neighborhood to see.

One of our friends ran to our house and told De-De. She ran outside and saw his dead body lying in his own blood. She fell on top of her lover's body and fainted right there. The death was tragic for our entire neighborhood because we all loved him, despite his lifestyle.

De-De was devastated about the death of her first love. We all went to Shorty's sad funeral, along with most of the people in the neighborhood. When it was time for De-De to view his body, she looked down at Shorty's lifeless body and screamed, "Why did you leave me Shorty? Take me with you! Don't leave me here!" My sister tried to jump into the casket, leaving half of her body inside of the casket. The casket rocked back and forth, as people gasped watching the casket sway. De-De and the casket almost fell to the floor. It scared me to think about the imminent crash which was about to happen. I could not move my legs or was I able to speak. The pall bears ran just in time to save her and the dead body from falling out of the casket. One of the ball bearers scooped her up in his arms and took her outside to calm her down. I just stood in shock and disbelief at how distraught she was. Even though the funeral was tragic, when we got home, we still laughed at how De-De got in the casket and almost fell as the casket rocked back and forth.

From that day on, Lenora's mother never went back outside. Lenora told me that it was too painful for her mother to see the spot where her son was killed. She stayed in her house and drank alcohol, day in and day out. Tragically, one year later, she died too.

After the incident, my mind went back to leaving and going to a university. I often thought about how Lenora met a fine young man when they attended the same university in Manhattan. I was so impressed with them. He was a great looking guy, light-skinned, bi-racial with deep black wavy hair. The girls in the neighborhood said that he was yummy to look at. He was a musician who played the bass guitar.

Lenora and I continued clubbing together and she introduced me to her friends. One friend she made sure to introduce me to was Boe Law. "Boe, this is my friend Vilma," she said. When I looked at that man, time stood still and the music stopped. What I saw was a handsome specimen of a man standing directly in front of me. I stood there with my mouth wide open staring at him. I looked him over from the top of his head, all the way down to his shoes. He had a nice and neat haircut, with a round-shaped head, and that caramel smooth skin. Handsome and serious, he looked like a sophisticated college man. He was wearing a long beige-colored wool coat, adorned with a suit and tie to match. I had not seen a man with a suit and tie on since the maître d on our vacation with Aunt G at the Waldorf Astoria. Oh God! I looked at his shoes, and saw they were shiny and new.

He stood at the bar like a celebrity. Again, I had never seen a man that looked as good as he did. "Hi Vilma," he said. "My name is Charles Law, but my friends call me Boe." He said my name like it was sweet to his mouth. When he spoke his name, I felt chills hit my body, which I had never felt before. *What was happening to me?*

"Vilma. What a pretty name for a pretty lady. What would you like to drink Vilma?"

I did not know what to order. "You choose for me," I

responded. That was something I heard Marilyn Monroe say on television, when offered a drink. He chose a drink called a slow gin fizz. *Mmm,* I thought, *sounds good and sweet.* I smiled my Marilyn Monroe smile and said, "Thank you." The drink was tasty and made my head spin a little. I was feeling happy and free.

I left Boe at the bar and went to the dance floor, hoping that he would follow. I wanted him to see how well I danced. But, he did not join me on the dance floor. Nevertheless, I danced to the sweet sounds of Donna Summer all night and talked with Boe. After I got tired of dancing, Boe asked me in a slow, sexy tone, "How old are you babe?" *Babe? It sounded oh so sweet.*

"Eighteen," I lied without even blinking. Boe handed me a card with his phone number and address on it.

"Call me sometimes babe." I appreciated that he gave me his phone number. I was just grateful that someone paid attention to me and the words were not negative. With just that, I about lost all sensibility. I had such a great night. I went home with Boe Law on my mind and planned to call him as soon as possible. I was all nerves, because I had never called a man before. I got up the next day ready to dial his number. I was hoping none of my sisters were around to hear me call him. When he answered the phone, I did not know what to say.

"Boe here."

"Hi Boe."

"Who is this?"

"Vilma. We met last night. Lenora's friend?"

"Hi babe. What you want?"

"I am just calling to say hi."

Well, hi babe."

"Are you going to the club Saturday night, Boe?" I hoped he did not hear in my voice that I was nervous and desperate to see him.

"I don't know."

"If you go Boe, can I meet you there?"

"That's up to you babe."

"Thank you Boe. See you there."

"Bye babe. I'm busy now."

Oh, he gave me chills. I was smiling from ear to ear. I had heard from my boyfriend, Boe. Could I have been more desperate? My self-esteem was so low that any nice words that a man gave made me think that I was his girlfriend. When one does not receive love at home, you will seek it out any way that you can get it. Everyone needs love, but it is extremely important to seek for real love. My lack of self-esteem gave Boe more power over me. He was an experienced man. I am sure he understood after that phone call that I was naive and young with low self-esteem.

I was on pins and needles excited to go back to the club on Saturday night to meet Boe again. I was going to dress sexy so he would not want to look at anyone else in the club. Saturday night finally came. I did not see Lenora, because she was out of town. I took the train to Manhattan by myself and left home around eleven pm. Besides, the club was not jumping until around midnight. I walked in and spotted Boe. He was standing at the bar talking to another woman who looked older than me. They were smiling like they knew each other.

Boe glanced in my direction, and then turned his attention back to the woman he was talking to. He did not even acknowledge me. I did not know what to do or how to approach him. My heart sank and I did not understand what was going on. I thought it may have been too dark in the club for him to see me. I decided to go to the restroom to compose myself, but upon my return, he was gone.

I decided to leave the club and visit the address on the card he gave me when we first met. When I arrived at his apartment complex, I was impressed. Believing he lived by himself, I started daydreaming about us living together in that complex.

I stood outside for a while. But because I was afraid to ring the doorbell, I went home. I thought I was in love. I didn't know because I never had a boyfriend before. The next day I called him and he did not answer his phone. I continued to call until I reached him.

"Hi Boe."

"Yes, what is it girl?"

"I just wanted to see how you were doing," I said.

He answered coldly, "Fine. What do you want?"

"I want you to come to my house Friday night."

"Sure," he said and hung up.

Early Saturday morning I was asleep, and at 2:00 am in the morning, the doorbell rang. My sisters and I lived on the third floor, so I looked out the window and it was Boe! I was excited to my delight that he showed up. I brought him to my tiny room. The only furniture that could fit in my room was a bed and dresser. He looked around my room with a surprised look of disappointment. I did not care; I was happy to see him. I disregarded the expression of disappointment on his face. I never had a boy in my room, but this was a man. I had no idea what I was supposed to do, say, or think. I tried to follow his lead. He was not talking. He laid me on my bed and we kissed. Then he took off my clothes. I was sweating and nervous. I had not been in bed with a man before. Still, he said nothing.

I laid down while he kissed me. I wondered about what was about to happen. I thought about Aunt G and how she had me sheltered and protected me. I was surprised she had not shown up yet, plus I was hoping that she would. I was not sure about what was going on and did not know how to stop it. I forced myself to stop thinking about her. *This is my time with my man,* I said to myself.

He began to unzip his pants, as I heard the zipper going up and down quickly. All of a sudden, I heard him moan loudly, like he was in pain. I thought, *what is he doing?* I did not feel anything, but became aware quickly that his penis got stuck in his zipper! Inexperienced, I was in shock and scared. *What was I supposed to do to? Help?* I felt bad and ashamed. I did not move as he struggled to free himself. When he finally freed himself from the zipper, he was angry about what happened. But his only interest was to get what he came for.

He proceeded to put his manhood inside of me. I revealed to him that I was a virgin. On top of me, he looked down and sighed, "God, girl! Who you been saving it for, Jesus?" He had no compassion whatsoever for what I revealed to him. He shoved his manhood in my vagina without one thought for me. The pain was bad and it felt like my skin was being ripped and torn. I found no pleasure in the entire ordeal. When he finished, he got up and left without even saying goodbye.

I laid there in my bed, numb not knowing how I was supposed to feel. It was nothing like I imagined it would be. *Why did I even invite him over? Were we supposed to be having sex?* I thought I would feel great, see stars and be warm and tingly all over. The next day I called Boe, but he did not answer his phone. I called him all week because I needed to talk to him. Besides, I thought I loved him.

One evening, my father, surprised me with a visit. We sat on the couch and watched television together for hours. I was glad that he and Aunt G did not fuss with each other. Then, we heard a knock at the door." "Who is it?" John asked? In walked Boe, with that same beautiful long coat on from the club. He walked in like he owned the place. Big John asked, "Who are you, and why are you here at nine o'clock at night to see my daughter?"

"Boe is my name."

"Is that your whole name, Boe?"

"Boe Law."

"How old are you, Boe Law?"

"Twenty-five."

"Twenty-five?!" John raised his voice. "Do you know how old my daughter is?"

"Yes, eighteen."

"You're an eighteen lie. She is seventeen years old and you are an old man! Are you planning on going to jail for statutory rape, Mr. Boe Law?"

"No!" Boe barked angrily.

The room grew silent. My heart was beating fast and I could only hope they did not hear it. I stood in one spot waiting for what would happen next. I was numb and in a *fog* without anything to say, praying that this would all go away soon. Boe stormed out of the house. But, Big John turned his attention to me. "You do know what he came he for tonight right? He is a man and every man want sex." I looked at Big John disappointed and went to my room. He left as well.

I missed my period for the month and my thoughts raced. *What's wrong with me? I can't be pregnant; I only had sex one time.* I had not seen or heard from Boe since the altercation with Big John. *What was I going to do?*

"Vilma, the doctor is ready to see you. Congratulations young lady you are pregnant!"

Oh, no! This is the worst thing that could happen to me. More racing thoughts came. *What am I going to do? Who could I talk to?* Aunt G will kill me and put me out of the house. All the way home on the bus, I tried to think about what to do. *Let me call Boe; he will help.* I called him but all I heard was the sound of the phone ringing which sounded like doom and gloom to me. No answer.

I took the bus to Boe's house and rung the bell until he came out to meet me. "What you are doing here, little girl? You did not tell me you were only seventeen."

"Sorry Boe," I said in a childlike manner, as I held my head down in shame. "I am in trouble; I am pregnant."

"So, what you want me to do?"

"We can get a place together and have a family."

Laughing, he said, "You are crazy little girl." He reached into his pocket. "Here is some money; take care of it."

"Take care of what Boe?"

"Girl, you are naïve! Get an abortion! I have too much to do than to fool around with you and a baby. I am about to complete law school. I have great plans for my life which does not include a little ghetto girl." He looked me straight in my face and said, "Now go and do not come back ever!"

Sobbing, I left. I called my Aunt Eatty, my mother's sister. She did not talk to my mother or accepted my mother as her sister.

She treated Mama just like my Gra Mother did, with contempt. She was the only person I could think to call. I told her that I was pregnant and that I needed some help. "Eatty, what am I going to do? I did not know who else to call."

"I can't help you," she laughed. "I don't know what you are going to do. Get off my phone."

It broke my heart to hear those words from her. Why did she refuse to help me? Aunt Eatty sound like she was glad to hear that I was in trouble. I began to wonder why I was attracted to Boe, but had no genuine answer. Was it his handsome looks or fine clothing? The fact is that he reminded me of my father. It was the way my father did not smile and the coldness in his personality. I saw those characteristics in Boe. But how could I be attracted to someone who was not nice to me? My attraction was an idea of a man. My absent father was the only example I had. I did not know what a good man was supposed to be like.

Today, I would say I should have learned to stay focused. But how? How does a 17-year-old with no one to respect her or teach the value of focus do that? How would I have known not to allow anyone to disrespect me, when I was repeatedly berated by my Aunt G? She did love me, but respect? Well, that wasn't in a large supply at our home. Guidance or self-love, I didn't receive. I wish I had not given away the most sacred part of myself. Still, I am grateful for the lessons learned. It took a while for me to learn that I was valuable and worthy of love *and* respect.

After the conversation with my Aunt Eatty, I felt hopelessness. I sat on the couch, watching television when a commercial came on. It was no ordinary commercial; they were talking about choices people had during pregnancy. The company was called Planned Parenthood.

Many thoughts raced through my mind. I did not want to be pregnant. Aunt G said if one of us got pregnant, we had to leave her house and I had nowhere to go. After watching the commercial, I scheduled an appointment.

I was quiet and sad, all the way to the clinic. The thought of having a child did not compute for me. I could not do it. As I stepped off the bus, I saw an extensive line of protestors in front of the building as I entered. They were chanting, "Stop killing innocent blood!" I saw signs, not sure what they were talking about. *Who was killing innocent babies?* As early as I was in my pregnancy, it was not a baby, that's what I heard. I made up my mind, what I was going to do. As I approached the waiting room, I felt a cold chill hit my body and almost fainted. I shook myself, to snap back and continue to stand. *Come on back Vilma,* I spoke to myself.

A nurse wearing all white came out and greeted me. She talked to me about options; to have the baby or an abortion. I knew what I was there for. She took me to an all-white, backroom; the bed, sheets walls, and floor were all white. She told me to get undressed and lay down. The bed felt like I was laying on ice. I tried not to think about any of it.

"Are you ready?" the nurse asked. I shook my head yes as my heart pumped fast. I kept my eyes opened to see what they were doing to me. The doctor instructed me to open my legs and put them in stirrups. He proceeded to put a big cold instrument between my legs. He had no expression and did not speak or acknowledge me. The nurse held my hands and squeezed. She said, "Take a deep breath; this is going to hurt a bit." The doctor connected me to a machine and turned it on. It sounded exactly like a vacuum cleaner.

I felt it pulling the baby from my stomach. Yes, it was a baby. I knew it even if I had heard in the initial stages, it was not a baby. As the machine sucked and pulled, I felt strong cramps hit my stomach. I moaned a bit and the ordeal was over. They cleaned me up and sent me on my way. The big machine had sucked my baby from my stomach.

On the bus ride home, I felt weak, sick, and tired. I finally made it home, and went to bed. I was sick with cramps and heavy bleeding. I stayed in bed for four days and I did not talk to anyone. No one even noticed that I was sick. I felt so depressed and lonely. I just did not understand my emotions or the pain that I was feeling. Depressed over my decision, but I did not regret what I did. After four days, I felt better and got out of bed. I never mentioned to anyone what I had gone through. I eventually forgot about Boe and made myself forget about the baby and the abortion. Life just went on.

Chapter 22

Life Goes On

I attended a local college in Manhattan for business administration and also worked as a part-time sales clerk. One day after work, I picked up my clothes from the cleaners in my neighborhood. The clerk working the desk was handsome. He smiled at me and I smiled back. "What's your name?"

"Vilma," I said.

"You are pretty."

"Thank you, I responded. "What's your name?"

"Ritchie."

Ritchie was 6'2 inches tall, light- skinned with red hair, freckles and a beautiful smile. He had on black dressed pants and a crisp white shirt. I thought he was well dressed for a man in my neighborhood. I received my clothes and went home.

"Vilma, someone is here to see you!" De-De yelled. I went to the door and it was Ritchie.

Surprised, I stammered, "Hi. What are you doing here?"

"I came to see you Vilma, to ask you out."

"How did you know where I lived? Oh, that's right my address was on the cleaner's ticket."

"Would you like to go to the movies with me?"

"Ah, yes."

We went to the movies on a Friday night and started officially dating after that night. The next week, he took me to his apartment. While there, he kissed me and asked if I had ever had sex before. I lied and said no, I had not. Well, we had sex. It was okay, nothing special for me because I did not have any feelings for Ritchie. I just went along because I thought that's what people did when they dated.

Ritchie visited with me every weekend and we always ended up at his apartment. His behavior changed, and he started becoming demanding. All he wanted to do was to go to his apartment and have sex. We did not go on anymore dates. One night while we were together, someone knocked on his door.

"Let me in Ritchie!" the voice said. "I know you are in there with another woman!"

"What?! Who is that?" I asked him.

"Shut up! It's my ex-girlfriend." he said.

She banged on that door for an hour. The more she banged, the more nervous I became. I wanted to leave his apartment, but Ritchie would not let me leave. So I stayed until the next morning. I made up in my mind that night that I did not want to see him anymore.

On my way home from work the next evening, I saw him. "Hi," he said, but I ignored him and went home. I then realized, I had left my high school class ring at his apartment. I called Ritchie and asked if he had seen my ring. But he denied seeing it. Instead, he asked me to go out with him again. "I am not going back to your apartment," I told him. Why didn't you tell me you had a girlfriend?"

"You didn't ask, he said, and she is my ex-girlfriend." That was a good lesson for me to always ask whether someone is dating someone else before going out with them.

The very next day as I was walking home, someone was calling my name. It was Ritchie's ex-girlfriend. I did not know her, but she knew me. She said someone in the neighborhood told her about me. She was obviously pregnant, and it looked like she was having twins. We talked about Ritchie and she said that they had been dating for three years. She told me she was pregnant with his twins.

I felt bad about the situation and went to find Ritchie. When I met up with him, he was on his way to his mother's house. He invited me to go and I went with him. We arrived at his mother's house and hadn't made it inside before they began screaming at each other. His mother appeared to be afraid of him. She backed up and people were staring at us. Ritchie was high. I found out through his mother that he used cocaine and alcohol. As bad as my mother was, I would never curse her out like that. Shoot as bad as Aunt G was, I dared not talk back to her. I thought anyone that talked to their mother like he did was dangerous. After that encounter, I was afraid of him

The incident with Ritchie and his treatment of women put a bad taste in my mouth about men. I saw him for who he was, a disturbed man. How could anyone have a mother and treat her badly? I thought about my mother and how I wished she was well enough to live with us. My heart broke for his mother, while my mother was in the Brooklyn New York State Institution for the Mentally Ill. My mother would not stop walking the streets and hearing voices, so Aunt Gail had her committed.

I told Ritchie that I was not going to see him again. He said okay, but we still went back to his place. I told myself that I wanted to try to find my high school ring. I don't know what I was expecting when I went back. But my ring was just that important to me. I worked hard to get it and I did not own anything else that was of value to me. I walked into the bedroom looking for my ring, and he followed me. I saw him lock the door behind himself and that did not sit well with me.

"What are you locking the door for, Ritchie?" I asked?

"You are not leaving here until you decide to stay with me."

"Well I guess we will be here for a long time because I am not staying with you."

As I reached for the door, Ritchie hit me in my face and knocked me down to the floor. "What is wrong with you?" I screamed. I remembered Aunt G always said, "If a man hits you, try your best to kill him." I hit him back with all my might. I tried to get to the door, but he had it locked. We wrestled for what seemed like hours.

When we were not wrestling, Ritchie was getting high on cocaine. His tirade went on the entire time he had me locked in his apartment. He was snorting cocaine, acting crazy, hitting, and cursing me. That was the first time I saw him take drugs. It was rumored that my boyfriend was a coke-head and violent. His own mother even had told me. I knew he drank a lot, but seeing it firsthand frightened me. He was raving and cursing about how women made him sick. "You all want a man, but when you get one, you don't know what to do with him! I am going to kill me somebody today!"

I was stuck at Ritchie's apartment all weekend trying to get away, fighting with him. I knew I had to get out of there and for good. He finally got tired of fighting with me, because I refused to stop fighting him. Finally, I found an opening to be free. Ritchie was bending over to get a hit of drugs, and I hit him with a stick that was in the room. Luckily, he passed out. Weak from hunger and my hands shaking, I got the key to the dead bolt from his pocket. As tears streamed down my eyes, I put the key in the keyhole. I looked back one last time at that crazy man, laying there, hoping I did not kill him. But I was grateful he did not move. I ran out of there as fast as I could.

Chapter 23

Home

I hailed a cab, arrived home early in the morning, and went straight to bed. As soon as I got into a deep sleep, Aunt G banged on my dang gone door. "Get up you riffraff! Are you going to sleep all day?" *Aunt G leave me alone*, I said in my mind. *I am not in the mood for your mess today.* I felt like I had just gone to bed. I had a rough few days with Crazy Ritchie and now here was Crazy Aunt G!

She demanded I let her in. "I am not letting you in here Aunt G. There's no one in my room but me."

"You don't have a room!" she yelled back. "I can go into any part of my house when I want to. I pay for everything in this house. Now let me in that room before I knock your head off!"

"Someone already tried that this weekend and failed!" I hollered back.

"Now here you come talking crazy. I am so tired of crazy people around me, I don't know what to do."

"Aunt G go away. I am tired."

"Tired from what?" She was in the room now. I had never in my life talked back to Aunt G before. Something on the inside of me was fed up. Something inside of me wanted a change from all the craziness. My insides were screaming for freedom. My insides were screaming for peace. I felt powerful for the first time in my life. I believed I could make it on my own. I was ready to take on Aunt G. I knew at that moment that I had to get away from her. I had to leave before I lost my courage. I needed to make a move before I did something bad and hurt someone.

As she normally did, she went on with her words of war. "If you are in my house, I can go through any room that I want to and when I want to. I paid for everything in here, including you. I get money for you and your sisters every month. You don't tell me what part of my house I can go in, or what part I cannot go in!"

Aunt G got closer in my face as she was talking. "If you don't like it, leave; this is not your forever home!" Those words hit me like a bulldozer. They hit my heart and head at the same time. *This is not your forever home. Where was my forever home, Lord?* The words rang in my ears, until I got dizzy.

Aunt G went on, "You can just leave! This is not your house; it's mine."

Before I could think, the words, "I am leaving now" came out of my mouth. "I am tired of you and all this mess, Aunt G. You said you had money for me when I was ready to move, let me have it! I am leaving!"

"Pack your raggedy clothes and go!" she said.

I could not dial the phone fast enough. I called a friend who had moved to Maryland two years earlier. Before my friend Tommy left New York, he gave me his phone number. He asked me to go with him to Maryland, but I was not ready to leave. Tommy had been in love with me since we were children. Tommy was an intelligent man. He was short in stature compared to the other boys in the neighborhood. Tommy often asked me out. One day I finally said, "Yes." We went for Chinese food. I ordered shrimp and rice and he ordered fried shrimp. We had a momentous time talking and laughing. I did not like Tommy romantically like he liked me. I saw us as just friends. Whenever I just needed a friend, I called him. After we ate our food we sat down together in my living room on the couch. When the moment was right, he kissed me. I leaned in to accommodate the kiss, but all I smelled was the fried shrimp on his breath. I got nauseous. I pushed him away, and ever since that day, whenever I saw him, all I could think about was his shrimp breath. Yuck!

"Hi, Tommy; how are you?"

"Well Vilma, good to hear from you."

"I was thinking about what you asked me before you left Tommy. You said that if I wanted to, I could come and live with you."

"Sure, I meant it Vilma."

"Well I am on my way. I cannot take this place anymore. Aunt G is driving me crazy and I have got to get out of here. I will get a job when I get out there."

"Okay Vilma. How will you be traveling?"

"Greyhound."

"Okay, I will meet you at the bus stop."

I packed a small bag of clothes and personal items. I planned to return later for the rest of my belongings. My sisters were sitting in the living room. "I am going to Maryland; I am moving out. Good-bye." I did not give an explanation; I did not know what to say to them. I did not think about their feelings or how my leaving affected them. I was thinking about myself. None of my sisters said anything except Shy. "Vilma don't go; I will miss you."

"I know Shy, but I must go. I promise to come back and see you as soon as I can." Aunt G came in the room handed me four hundred dollars and walked out of the room.

Chapter 24

Forever Home

I bought my one-way ticket to Baltimore, Maryland and boarded the bus. My emotions were up and down; I felt sad, yet ready. I did not know what to expect in Baltimore, but Tommy was waiting for me. I got a window seat on the bus and thought it was time for a change. I planned to get there and get an excellent job. I would get a new home since I had never had a real home before.

Having my own home was important to me. I was excited about being nineteen and learned, that I could make it, if I did not give up on myself. People will give up on you, but do not give up on yourself or your dreams. Once we give up on ourselves, we turn the power over to someone else to control us. I planned to fight for the right to live well, even if it was to the death.

As I looked out of the window of the old dirty bus, it smelled like musk. I wondered what life was about to give me. I looked for hope and happiness. I had a renewed state of mind, to do better in my life. I just did not know what to expect. I concentrated on the new possibilities that were out in Maryland. I made up in my mind that no matter what happened in this next chapter of life, I would not look back. I would never move back to Aunt G's house. She controlled me all my life, but now my life belonged to me. It was up to me to make the most out of it.

I had suffered a lot, been in a great state of fogginess since I could remember. I had seen and heard much. My sisters and I were homeless. I was rejected by my mother, father, and others who considered me nothing. I knew that I was different. I had always felt that I was different from others in the family. Most of my life had been a big daydream. I was always dreaming of a happier life.

Leaving, I did not feel scared. My heart was pumping real and new blood. I felt the excitement of new life and new breath. No matter what happened, I was hopeful. We must have hope. We must keep dreaming that there is a way out of all undesirable things. There is a force stronger than us.

In my heart, I believed that God had a plan for me. I believed that there was greatness for me. I knew I would see my sisters and I reunited again. I was not strong, or ready to help them now. But I believed that there was a way out for them as well. I had no fear, no worries, a new life, and a new home. Trusting that everything would be fine, I believed I could make it.

As the wheels on the bus moved me into new life, I reviewed the physical torment of my sisters. We were treated less than dogs. I was told by many of my relatives I would never amount to anything. Now, I believed that I was going to make it. I believed that I was special to someone. I knew without a shadow of a doubt, that I was put on earth to help others to make it out of their tormented times. There was a real home somewhere for me and I was going to find my forever home.

Meet the Author

Lorraine Jenkins-Wilkes resides in North Carolina with her husband of ten years and have three adult children combined. She uses laughter in tough life situations and has believed in the healing power of laughter. Employed in the healthcare field for over thirty years, Lorraine is a Chaplain/Counselor for a large healthcare corporation, possessing a certification as a Certified Assisted Living Administrator. Moreover, she currently serves as a licensed ordained pastor and inspirational domestic abuse speaker. She has earned a bachelor's degree in theology and two associates in healthcare. She is the visionary and host of the non-profit Christian talk show entitled "The Power of S.H.E."

Her calling in life was birthed through the price of living through trauma of rejection, and abuse, along with witnessing her mother being institutionalized at an early age. Her vision in life is to help those stuck in their past hurts, to survive and thrive with the help of the Lord Jesus Christ. Lorraine's prayer for her memoir is that it will pull the cover off domestic abuse and help others to be completely whole in every area of life, like it is still doing for her and her sisters. This book will help through the process of peeling away trauma and memories of abuse. I pray as you read this book you will find your freedom to be open. *10% of book proceeds will be donated to benefit the Coalition against Domestic Violence.*

For booking information for her speaking ministry and to purchase "Forever Home":

Lorraine Jenkins-Wilkes
P.O. Box 815
Elm City, NC 27822

Email: powerofshe123@gmail.com

Website: www.Lorrainejenkinswilkesforeverhome.com

Facebook: The Power of S.H.E.

Instagram: The Power of S.H.E.

YouTube: PowerofSHE